WHATEVER HAPPENED TO THE CHURCH?

By
Rayola Kelley

Hidden Manna Publications

Whatever Happened to the Church?
Copyright © 2008 and 2025 by Rayola Kelley

GENTLE SHEPHERD MINISTRIES
www.gentleshepherd.com

ISBN: 979-8-9994555-5-0

Except where otherwise indicated, all Scripture quotations in this book are taken from the King James Version of the Bible.

Hidden **M**anna **P**ublications
P.O. Box 3572
Oldtown, ID 83822
www.gentleshepherd.com

Facebook:
https://www.facebook.com/HiddenMannaPublications/

Contents

INTRODUCTION

One of the questions that many Christians struggle with is, "Whatever happened to the Church?" This haunts many of God's saints as they find themselves searching for some type of sanity in Christendom. As they go from one church to another, they seem to find broken cisterns of man's religion and influence, poison waters of heresy, stagnant pools that are lifeless, and the endless mixture of worldly influences and perversion taking center stage in many of the attitudes and practices that are going on in the name of Christianity.

In this book I am going to attempt to answer this question. To be perfectly honest with you, I have also struggled with this issue. As I have waded through the many challenges that seem to plague the Christian Church, I have been accused of being too negative or even as being against the Church. Such accusations are false. However, what I have discovered is that what is now considered to be the Church has been cleverly redefined according to worldly or erroneous attitudes and mindsets that are firmly in place, causing confusion for many in the Christian realm. Even though Scripture is clear about the makeup of the Church that Jesus died for, it appears as if many within Christendom have been conditioned by a counterfeit presentation.

My desire is to establish the real meaning of the Church in light of how it has been cleverly redefined. In so doing, I hope to set the seeking heart free from the torment and struggle that is going on among so many of God's people.

Keep in mind that we are about to take a journey through the struggles of the Church. These struggles are not new. What many saints are experiencing now also challenged the new Church. What the watchmen contended with in the first centuries of the Church, and throughout its history, happens to be the very same issues the present-day watchmen are trying to expose, warn against, and bring proper instruction about to God's people. Granted, these issues may have been repackaged to fit our modern-day palates of higher criticism, the psychology of the world, and the endless bombardment of useless entertainment and humanistic philosophies, but the issues remain the same.

Although some people might consider this book discouraging, they will also discover that the Church that Jesus Christ died for stills exists. It may be hidden, discarded, persecuted, rejected, and mocked, but it is still very much alive, even in the midst of the great darkness that is engulfing the present age.

Let us now begin this journey to discover the true face of the blood-bought Church of the Lord Jesus Christ.

Part I

LAYING
A
FOUNDATION

1

WHAT IS THE CHURCH?

My initial religious exposure and influence came from a cult. Although this cult appeared to have attractive presentations in its various stands regarding family and moral issues, it was all simply a front that had no spirit or life. This was obvious, as I had to constantly face the harsh reality of the besetting sins that confronted my family and me.

These constant struggles were shrouded by unrealistic religious standards and demands that, all too often, exposed hypocrisy in the lives of my family and the other cult members that I was personally acquainted with. It was clear that the standards of this cult did not empower its members or provide a sustaining anchor that would bring lasting hope.

I never thought much about whether the religion of my cult was genuine. In my younger years, I was not really concerned about such issues. However, I would learn that such matters would eventually be challenged, tested, or even shaken.[1] Such challenges would sometimes penetrate the indifference of my immaturity to cause me to consider if there was some type of absolute truth to matters of life and death that surrounded the issues of God that I needed to discover for myself.

When I was a teenager, I encountered such a challenge. My mother was talking about religious matters to my stepfather's

---
[1] Hebrews 12:27

mother, who I also fondly considered to be my grandmother. Since I was in the vicinity, I was listening to what was being said. My mother, who was doubtful about the cult because of unanswered questions and suspicions, was sharing some of her feelings. My grandmother made a statement that penetrated both my mother and me. She stated that the true Church was not made up of buildings, denominations, or organized religious systems. Rather, it was actually made up of people.

The idea that the real Church was made up of people went into my spirit. It seemed strange because I had always identified "church" as a "building" that promoted religious beliefs and practices. However, the idea that the Church was not made up of lifeless buildings or indifferent doctrines made sense to my spirit. I would later learn it was all about being conditioned to perceive a certain way.

As I look back upon that time, I realize my indifferent spirit was actually being stirred by the definition of the true Church. This challenge started a small fascination in me concerning the possibilities of God and His real Church. The fact that His Church was actually comprised of people who somehow understood what it meant to believe, love, and serve Him made God appear less indifferent. In a way, it served as a key that would slowly unlock a door that would lead me to the salvation of my soul.

When I became a Christian, one of my goals was to understand the real makeup of the Church that Jesus died for. Obviously, this very Church had to be established in Spirit and truth. I wanted to see if what my grandmother had originally said about the Church was true. If it was true, I sensed that so much of the indifference or vagueness that caused me to see God as impersonal was not only incorrect, but it was a product of the religious state of ignorance that was clearly in operation in the cult that was influencing my family and me.

Such a revelation about my misconceptions about God being indifferent caused me to realize how personal He can be if allowed, and how He desires to meet with His people and be involve with their welfare. It would also mean that He does not use the means of buildings, denominations, and even doctrines to identify and meet with those who belong to Him.

It is from this premise that I am approaching the subject of what makes up the true Church. It is important that we identify what is actually considered the true Body of Christ for the purpose of understanding what has happened to it in the twenty centuries since it was born and brought forth by the Holy Spirit and in truth. If we fail to start from the proper premise, we will never understand the identity crisis that the Church has been struggling with throughout the years.

This identity crisis is nothing new. In fact, in many cases, it has served as the refining fires that have caused the true Church to come forth with distinction, purpose, and renewed commitment and vision. In such testing, the real Church has always emerged distinct, peculiar, and separate from what is considered normal and acceptable by the masses.

Such separation is the real key behind resolving the identity crisis that is shaking many within the Church. The true Church must understand its authority, purpose, and power if it is going to come back to its roots and the place that God has designed for it in His kingdom.

Once we, as believers, understand the design that God unveiled in Scripture in regard to His true Church, we will understand what it will take for it to be established according to the heavenly design. Once the Church is reestablished or realigned according to God's design, this entity will understand what it will take to function in light of His plan. This means the Church will take its rightful place in His kingdom.

In studying the Scriptures about the Church of Christ, I found that my grandmother was correct. We are told that those who truly believe in the Lord Jesus Christ for their salvation make up His Church.[2] Clearly, God meant the Church to be a living organism.

The Church would serve as the Body of Christ, while Jesus served as the Head of the Church. As the Head, all life and functions of the Body would originate or come from Him. In this Body, God would individually place each member by way of baptism of the Holy Spirit, for we are told that the Holy Spirit is the One who baptizes each member into this incredible Body. The members of this entity would be equal in importance, distinct in their places and function to ensure the effectual working of the whole Body. Obviously, God is the One who will temper this Body together for His use and glory.[3]

The Church would serve as a living building. We know that God is building this house, but He has placed Christ, as a Son, over it. A house reminds us that it is meant to be a dwelling place. The Word of God makes it clear who will dwell in this incredible house when it speaks of each believer as being a temple of the Holy Spirit. Clearly, the Church will be serving as a residence for God in the midst of this world.[4]

This brings us to the activities that must take place in this spiritual house of God. The Apostle Peter is the one who gave us insight into this matter. He first described believers as lively stones that have been used to build up a spiritual house. As a spiritual house, we as believers will be subject to the Spirit and not to the ways of the flesh or the world. Peter went on to stipulate that the Church not only represents a spiritual house, but it also comprises a holy priesthood. Each believer is also a priest. As priests of this

---

[2] Ephesians 4:11-16; Colossians 1:18
[3] 1 Corinthians 12:12-26
[4] 1 Corinthians 3:9, 16-17; 6:19-20; Hebrews 3:4-6

spiritual house, we are to offer spiritual sacrifices, acceptable to God by Jesus Christ.[5]

The Apostle Peter also informed us that we are a chosen generation, a royal priesthood, and a holy nation of peculiar or special people that belong to God. As a chosen generation, we have been marked and set apart to represent God in this world. As a royal priesthood, we are reminded that, as part as the building of the Church, we have royal ties to an eternal King and kingdom, and we are here to represent God to man and man to God. Of course, as priests, we perform devoted service in God's house and to His people under the ever watchful, caring auspice of our High Priest: Jesus Christ.[6]

The Church is also a holy nation. This again points to separation. We may be in the midst of this world with its many kingdoms and nations, but we are not part of it. We have a separate king, law, mission, and lifestyle that we live in accordance to. This high calling and position in Christ will also bring us into agreement with the intent and purpose of our King. As a result, we will stand distinct from the rest of the world.

The Church would become the harvest field of God. As His field, we must be cultivated. The Father is the true husbandman of our lives. He must, through the working of the Spirit, plough up the fallow ground of our hearts so that the seed of His Word can take root. He allows the north wind of trials to challenge our faith, but He also sends the gentle south breezes to bring forth new life. Under His watchful eyes, each season of regenerating, growing, purging, harvesting, and dying to the former beauty gives way to a deeper work in our hearts.[7]

As believers, we experience a deeper work during each cycle of these different spiritual seasons. In the springtime, the life of

---

[5] 1 Peter 2:5
[6] Hebrews 7:17-28; 1 Peter 2:9
[7] Song of Solomon 4:16; Jeremiah 4:3-4; Matthew 13:1-23; 1 Corinthians 6:9

Christ is established in us in greater ways, unfolding a beauty that is virtuous and lasting. In the summer, the heat will purge that which is not of God, as bits of the flesh and pride wither under the penetrating heat of trials. In spite of the challenge of each season, the harvest is eventually reaped. However, the fruits that come forth must be the extension of the Vine of Jesus Christ.[8]

It is God's desire to take the barren wilderness of man's heart and soul and make it into a wondrous garden. In this garden, we, as believers, are being planted as trees by the rivers of water. As His saints, we will be established in righteousness for the purpose of bringing forth acceptable fruit.[9]

In this garden are a variety of flowers. These different plants point to us as His saints, reflecting the glory of our Lord as the fragrance of His life in us reaches the throne of God. Although the outward beauty of our flesh will eventually fade, the inward beauty will be constantly renewed and established by the working of the Holy Spirit. It is in this garden of our hearts that sweet communion takes place.[10]

Once the husbandman has established His garden in our inner man, we must pull up our sleeves and put our shoulders to the plough. God is calling us to be co-laborers with Him in the harvest field of humanity. His whole goal for working in the harvest field of our lives is to bring forth fruit. This fruit points to the very life of Christ being multiplied in others.

The Apostle Paul talked about how some servants plant the seeds of Jesus' life through the preaching of the Gospel and how others water the seeds through the work of making disciples. The key to being fruit-bearing Christians is that others will become attracted to Jesus by the fruit of our lives.[11]

---

[8] John 15:1

[9] Psalms 1:3; Proverbs 11:30; Song of Solomon 4:12, 16

[10] Psalms 103:14-1; Isaiah 58:11; 2 Corinthians 2:15-16; 3:18; 4:16; James 4:14; 1 Peter 1:24

[11] Luke 9:62; John 15:5-8; 1 Corinthians 3:6-8; Galatians 5:22-23

There is a debate over who is the Bride of Christ. Some believe it will be Israel, while others believe it is the Church. Jesus told the disciples that He was preparing a place for them.[12] According to the culture at that time, those who were espoused were considered married. However, the bridegroom had to first prepare a place for his bride before the marriage could be consummated. It was the father of the bridegroom who decided when this place was acceptable for the bridegroom to bring his bride home.

It is obvious that, as the heavenly matchmaker, the Holy Spirit has sought out those who will become part of the Body. He has wooed all who have been drawn to the Son by exalting Him, leading saints into all truth about His character and commitment. He has been sanctifying them with the linen clothes of righteousness.[13]

The debate over this issue of the Bride of Christ may prove to be unprofitable. The marriage supper of the Lamb will take place. Clearly, the Church is the Body; therefore, the Body is going to be where the Head is. Right now, the Head is not physically present, but, one day, Jesus is going to come for His Church. Whether He comes in the capacity of the Head or the Bridegroom, we, as believers, will be raised up with resurrection power to meet Him in the air.[14]

We know that, as Jesus' Body, His Word is cleansing us. We also know that only those wearing the proper garments will attend this most important supper.[15] Whether we are at the wedding supper of the Lamb because we are His Body or because we are part of the Bride, or both positions are intertwined together will probably seem immaterial when we are actually in His presence. We will simply rejoice because, as our Head, we will clearly be

---

[12] John 14:1-3
[13] John 16:13-14; Romans 15:16
[14] 1 Thessalonians 4:13-18; Revelation 19:7-10.
[15] Matthew 22:10-14; Ephesians 5:26-27

united with Him once and for all. And, if Israel solely serves as the Bride, we will be rejoicing that all matters have been completed according to the covenant and plan of the Father.

Obviously, the Church must humbly submit to this glorious preparation that must take place. All weddings have invitations and the marriage supper of the Lamb is no exception. There is an invitation that has gone out, and each person needs to accept it. Hear the invitation, *"And the Spirit and the bride say, Come. And let him that heareth say, Come. And let him that is athirst come. And whosoever will, let him take the water of life freely"* *(Revelation 22:17).*

Those of the Church must daily come to the source of life to be refilled, refreshed, and renewed. They must come to Jesus and partake of the Living Water that will constantly spring up into eternal life. As part of the Body, we must each sit at the table of communion and partake of the divine nature of Jesus to be established in His life by faith. We must come to be washed by the water of the Word and cleansed from all unrighteousness by His blood.[16]

Today many of God's sheep are being scattered because they cannot hear the voice of the Shepherd. They desire to come to the Living Water, but they encounter dry wells and muddied water. There are many invitations, but the tender voice and signature of the Spirit is missing. Therefore, the sheep continue to seek for the Shepherd who will lead them up the paths of righteousness to the still waters that renew and the green pastures that they are able to feed upon.[17]

This brings us to what distinguishes the real Church of Jesus from the counterfeits. It is alive. It is not an indifferent building, system, denomination, or doctrine. It is a living organism. It lives because of the Spirit that inspires and leads and the liberating

---

[16] John 4:10-14; 7:37-39; Ephesians 5:26; 2 Peter 1:3-4
[17] Psalm 23:1-3; John 10:1-11

truth that establishes it upon the immovable Rock. After all, it is the Spirit who leads believers to all truth about Jesus. It is the Spirit who will show the Church the things to come for preparation, and who serves as the true teacher to the Body.[18] Although the flame of life might appear weak in some of the Church and the resolve of some to cling to the Rock may be questionable, the Church lives. It has the eternal flame within it and the eternal Rock of ages to keep it.

The Church lives, and, one day, this extraordinary Body will be brought forth in the unhindered glory of the One who purchased her. There will be no doubt about her existence, witness, flame, or foundation. Her existence will be unveiled in His glory, her witness will be confirmed in a future reign with her Lord, her flame will become a consuming fire in light of His judgment, and her foundation will be standing when all others crumble as shifting sand beneath the storms of God's wrath.

The question is are you part of this living organism? If not, you need to receive the life of Jesus. You do this by humbling yourself before God, and saying a heart-felt prayer similar to this one.

Lord Jesus, You are the Son of the Living God, the Christ. You came in the flesh to meet all of us in our sinful, hopeless plight. In fact, You have invited all of us to come to You to receive Your life. I know I am a sinner separated from You, but I know You gave Your life so that I could live. I now come to You in need of forgiveness and salvation. Forgive me for my sins and have mercy upon my soul. Show me Your grace by giving me the gift of eternal life. By faith I accept Your pardon, in order to receive Your life, knowing that from this day forth I am a new creature, walking away from the old towards the new to receive all that You have for me. Amen.

---

[18] John 16:13; 1 John 2:27

2

A BIT OF HISTORY

As my family and friends know, I am not a professional historian. However, I believe one has to understand history in order to realistically evaluate the present with the intention of making sound decisions in light of the future. Therefore, it is important to consider the history of the Church in order to understand what has happened to it over the past two thousand years.

In order to think about the history of the Church, we need to regard it from the perspective of what has influenced or challenged it over the years. Obviously, we are not going to be caught up with dates, but with events or incidents that have challenged or changed its state.

This brings us to what must always be kept in mind in order to understand what happened to the Church, and that is the environment or disposition of the Church. Environment will determine the weaknesses and strengths of something. For example, the Church was persecuted off and on for the first two hundred years.

After years of persecution, the believers were weary. Although much of the Church had been refined through the persecution, its members wanted some relief or deliverance from the unpredictable waves of persecution that would come upon them. When Constantine supposedly had his vision that inspired him to make the whole known world Christian, the believers saw it as an answer to prayer. After all, the members were weary of withstanding the attacks from religion and the world.

However, Constantine was a test and not an answer to prayer. The Christian life is not legislated through declarations or laws, nor does it exist through some type of force or association, such as we see in the case of extreme, violent Islam practices. Rather, Christians are born again from above.

Such individuals must be drawn by the Father, hear and receive the invitation of the Son, and be convicted by the Holy Spirit about their need for salvation due to sin.[1] As one can see, this is a spiritual preparation that is done from above and not from worldly, fleshly, or legal attempts that come from man's best attempts to right the wrongs of the present world according to his personal take on matters.

Sadly, we see the same attempts taking place today. There are Christians who are trying to stop the moral decline of this nation through political avenues. However, this is clearly the world's way and not God's. We can see this in the case of Babylon.

The Israelites were told they needed to make their homes in godless Babylon because they would be in exile for 70 years. However, they were to pray for peace for the city in which they were held captive.

As Christians, we are told to pray for the leaders that we may also lead a quiet and peaceable life in all godliness and honesty. Clearly, as Christians, we do not have a mandate to become political activists. Don't get me wrong, we have a voice in the voting booth, but we need to be realistic about where our power and influence will rest. It will be on bended knees in our prayer closets, humbly seeking forgiveness and mercy for the wretched state of this nation and the professing Church.[2]

---

[1] John 3:3, 5; 6:44; 7:37; 16:7-11
[2] 2 Chronicles 7:14; Jeremiah 25:11; 29:4-7; 1 Timothy 2:2-3

Many in America also believe we are a Christian nation that God will somehow preserve and honor. This is not true. Keep in mind that God allowed His city, Jerusalem, and His temple to be destroyed because of sin. Granted, people such as Daniel and Ezekiel survived, but they were taken into captivity to serve foreign leaders.[3]

It is true that much of America is founded upon Judeo-Christian principles, which also makes it more accountable to the spiritual condition to which it succumbs. However, just because the establishment of our nation's foundation was influenced by those who understood that God's blessings were necessary for this nation to survive does not make it Christian.

The identifying mark of Christianity that must be seen is meant to identify individuals to the unseen kingdom of God. Granted, leaders set a tone for the moral attitude of a nation and the people are to maintain the integrity of it, but the term "Christian" describes individuals.

The mark that sets Christians apart and identifies them with the kingdom of God is the seal of the Holy Spirit. This seal identifies each of us as believers to an actual inheritance and endowment that will only be fully realized in light of the fullness of redemption and eternity. Since the Holy Spirit is the identifying mark, we must recognize that He can only be discerned spiritually, not recognized from the basis of the natural man.[4]

This brings us back to what happened to the Church in the fourth century. It was simple. Under the auspice of Constantine, it was organized into a religious system. This may not seem like a terrible blow to the Church, but, in a way, it was the beginning of the Church experiencing an identity crisis. In fact, the seeds that were planted ultimately produce what we now know as the Roman Catholic Church.

---

[3] Deuteronomy 28:36-37;
[4] 1 Corinthians 2:11-14; Ephesians 1:11-14; 1 John 2:20

The Church that Jesus died for was to function according to its Head, Jesus, and was to be led by the Holy Spirit in all spiritual matters. The members of this Body were to be fitted together by the Spirit according to the eternal plan of the Father. The idea of organizing this Body would appear to be quite logical to bring order. However, the order of the true Body of Christ was and is dependent upon it being in sync with the Head in its functions and responsibilities. If the Body is acting contrary to the Head, it will eventually discover that it is out of order, and it will become sick with ineffectiveness.

The question is how do you organize a living Body whose very life and functions are dependent on the Head and Spirit? You don't. All you can do is ensure the order of the present surroundings in order to establish a certain environment in which the Body can be properly influenced in the right way.

When man organizes a matter, it is often to control it in order to influence it according to his agendas. Clearly, such organization is meant to influence the minds of those who come under the auspice of such an association. In other words, such organizations will end up setting the premise of how people will perceive, evaluate, or judge a matter.

Until the fourth century, the Church may have faced persecution, but the members understood that they were an extension of the Head. They worshipped in one accord in places such as homes and catacombs. They would come together to partake of God's Word and commune together. They edified one another, as well as tarried before God in prayer. Such meetings were personal. After all, when one member of the Body suffered, the whole Body shared in that member's suffering. This is why the Apostle Paul talked about weeping with those who weep and rejoicing with those who were rejoicing.[5]

---

[5] Romans 12:15-16; 1 Corinthians 12:12, 26-27

When you consider that many Christians start from the premise of an organized church, you can begin to understand why the real identity of the Church is shrouded in confusion. Granted, we as Christians may know intellectually that the Church of Jesus is made up of blood-bought saints, but such understanding does not serve as the premise by which we naturally judge a matter. Without the right premise from which to evaluate the real makeup of the Church, we, as believers, will never possess a true revelation of it in our spirit.

It is important for us to understand that, when the Church comes under the auspice of man, whether it is through an organized effort or system, it becomes disconnected from the Head. Without this vital connection, the Body cannot function, and it will eventually lose all sense of its heavenly identity and inner life.

When you consider the apostles of the new Church, their main goal was to connect each member to the headship of Christ. The Apostle Paul instructed the Corinthian believers to follow him as he followed Christ. The Apostle Peter wrote to the Christians, reminding them of their humble beginnings. He told the pastors to humbly feed the sheep in light of facing the Chief Shepherd when He appears for His Body.[6]

If you are a Christian, the question is, are you connected to the Head? Is your life and purpose being inspired and motivated by love and devotion towards Jesus Christ? If it isn't, you are most likely feeling restless in your soul. You will sense something is missing, but you cannot quite figure it out. After all, you possibly go to church, pay tithes, and do good works, but none of it is really satisfying. In your mind, you are doing everything you can to be a good Christian, and yet it all appears to be empty. It simply does not make any sense.

[6] 1 Corinthians 11:1; 1 Peter 5:1-4; 2 Peter 1:4-12

Be sure to continue on to the next chapter to discover what could be missing from your spiritual life.

3

WHAT IS MISSING?

In the last chapter, we touched a bit on the history of the Church. It is important to note that the initial challenge for the new Church was to ensure the integrity and completion of God's Word. According to David W. Bercot in his book entitled *Will the Real Heretics Please Stand Up,* the leaders of this new Church had to wade through the heretical writings that were claiming validity and authority with the writings of such godly leaders as John, Peter, and Paul. As a result, the leaders of this new Body had to wade through the endless parade of counterfeit writings and letters. Sadly, the professing Church, which is quite visible and popular today, has embraced some of these very writings that the early fathers of the new Church clearly rejected and labeled as heretical.

These leaders had to become Bereans and test the spirit of these writings to see if they were in agreement with the complete spirit and intent of what had already been established as truth according to Scripture.[1] In order to ensure that the spirit lined up to the truth of God, these writings had to uphold and maintain the character and work of God. In order to make sure that they came into line with the intent of God's examples and plan of redemption, they had to uphold the will and ultimate purpose of God towards His people.

---

[1] Acts 17:10-12

The new Church understood that these counterfeits were after the minds of the vulnerable sheep of God. Once these heretical claims or teachings took the mind into captivity, the heart, with its devotion and affections, would naturally follow. In a sense, these leaders were fighting to maintain the integrity of the faith that was first entrusted to them by the first apostles of the new Church. No doubt, it was an intense battle that they could not and would not lose. After all, the Spirit would identify what He inspired, and the grace of God would give those committed saints entrusted with such a grave responsibility the necessary favor to see this solemn challenge through to the end.[2]

Within the first four centuries the Word of God had been established. In fact, the Church was in agreement with its validity and the type of authority it had to have in its life and function as the Body of Christ. As clearly stated within Scripture, it had to serve as the milk and meat to the very growth and survival of the Body.[3] It is hard to ignore the statement that Jesus made to Satan in the wilderness during His temptation, *"It is written, Man shall not live by bread alone, but by every word that proceedeth out of the mouth of God" (Matthew 4:4b).*

When Constantine came on the spiritual scene in A. D. 313, after he supposedly became a Christian, his vision to make his empire Christian, no doubt, appeared to be a Godsend to the battle-weary Body. As persecuted Christians, their sincere desire would be to seek a place of peace and liberty in which they could truly worship God. It seemed simple enough, but such relief usually comes with a price.

For example, the children of Israel had to be led out into the barren wilderness to worship God. For the pilgrims that first settled America, they had to give up what little they had in their present lives to pursue a new land of spiritual hope and opportunity to truly

---

[2] 2 Timothy 2:16; 2 Peter 1:19-21
[3] Hebrews 5:11-14

worship God. When they finally reached America after weeks of unbearable conditions and terrible storms, half of them lost their lives due to the adverse conditions that confronted them in the new land.

The problem with being offered something that appears to be too good to be true is that the intentions and hopes may be good, but the end results may be devastating. There is always some type of price attached to such presentations. The price attached to the concept that there could be a Christian empire was that it was nothing but a lie that was based on wishful thinking.

No doubt, my statement might surprise some of you. It may seem foreign to you, but the Word of God will bear it out. What many in the professing Church have forgotten is that we, as believers, make up a separate kingdom in this world, just as Israel makes up a separate nation. The Apostle Paul stipulated that we are citizens of heaven. We happen to represent this kingdom in this present world in the official capacity of ambassadors.[4]

The Apostle Peter referred to the Church or Body as a holy nation who was peculiar or special because its members belonged to God. Clearly, those who are members of this Body make up a kingdom that resides in the midst of other nations and kingdoms. This kingdom has one king over it. His name is Jesus Christ. The walls of buildings and the borders of this present world cannot contain this unseen kingdom that is realized in the hearts of believers and is universal in scope.[5]

Jesus said of His kingdom, *"My kingdom is not of this world; if my kingdom were of this world, then would my servants fight, that I should not be delivered to the Jews; but now is my kingdom not from here" (John 18:36b)*. Jesus was not saying that His kingdom was not *in* the world; rather, He was making it quite clear that it was not *of* the world. In other words, it would not belong to the

---

[4] 2 Corinthians 5:20; Philippians 3:20
[5] Mark 4:30-32; Luke 17:20-21; 1 Peter 2:9

world, be like the world, or have any part or agreement with the world. His kingdom would function separately from the nations of the world.

This brings us back to the lie that a nation or a kingdom of the world could be Christian. There may be Christian roots and foundations, which identifies the nation to a spiritual heritage or influence, but according to *2 Corinthians 4:3-4*, there is only one god and ruler that greatly influences the systems of this present world. We know this god and ruler to be Satan, not Jesus.

Granted, Jesus is coming back to rule over the nations of the world as King. The knowledge of the Lord will fill the earth at this time, and there will be both a moral and spiritual accountability that will discipline and bring all conduct into order. However, He does not rule over America as king, nor does He rule over any other nation of the world in this capacity, including Israel. Nations can be associated with the Judeo-Christian principles that can be seen in their laws and in honorable practices, but it does not necessarily make them Christian.

It has already been established that the unseen seal of the Spirit identifies believers with heaven. However, Jesus reigning in our hearts as Lord and King is what will visibly identify us with the kingdom of God. Christians are not only subject to Jesus as King in an official capacity, but He is also Lord. This means that they belong to Him and are called to be servants in His household.

With this understanding in mind, we can now begin to explore what happened to the Church. When the beleaguered Christians were willing to come under the auspice of a national leader, I am sure they did not understand the implications of their agreement. They were weary, meaning that their patience had been worn down. Sometimes such weariness will cause people to put down their guard when something that has the appearance of a viable solution is presented to them. We can probably conclude that they did not see themselves as giving up their autonomy under Christ to a worldly government. Perhaps, they saw themselves as simply supporting a Christian leader who was going to ensure their liberty to serve and worship God without fear of persecution.

We also might conclude that these believers did not see themselves as coming into agreement with any aspect of the world. However, Constantine may have been a professing Christian due to his vision, but, according to history, he did not live it. He was involved in immoral and abominable acts, which included the murder of family members. Based on the fruits of his attitude and conduct, we must consider whether he was simply Christian in name or association only.

Since Constantine was a leader over an empire, how would he institute the concept of a Christian nation or empire? After all, there were many pagans in his empire. He also held to some of those questionable religious practices and beliefs that had been part of his old pagan influences and practices.

According to E. H. Broadbent, in his book *The Pilgrim Church,* some of these beliefs and practices that Constantine held to can be traced back to the "Old Catholic Church" that was formed by Cyprian in the first part of the third century. Therefore, how would this ruler bring Christian influences together with idolatrous, pagan inspired beliefs and practices, while making them appear dutifully acceptable or a worthy addition to the masses? After all, Christians would consider those who were not of the faith as heathens or pagan in their practices. If there was any religion in the pagans' midst, it would be deemed idolatrous. Like many of the people today who hold to their old ways, such individuals generally do not care what belief others hold to, but they have no intention of giving up their own particular way of thinking or living.

Consider this environment. Constantine did not have an easy task. You cannot convince someone to be a Christian against their will. Such people may comply outwardly, while holding onto their old ways inwardly. They may appear honorable, but these individuals are still on their way to hell.

There was a similar situation in Samaria. The Assyrian army came into Israel and brought the people of Israel to their knees in utter defeat. The people of Israel were dispersed throughout the empire while Assyria brought in people from other areas to settle Samaria.

These people brought their gods and culture with them. However, the God of Israel was not pleased. He sent lions among them to slay them. The Creator of the universe clearly gained the attention of the inhabitants of Samaria. The inhabitants went to the king of Assyria and asked for the priest of Jehovah to be sent to them to teach them the manner of the God of Israel. As the story goes, a priest came. These people gladly took the information and instituted it into their different forms of idol worship. Needless to say, they defiled the things of God, but, in their minds, it was a way of keeping peace with Him.[6]

For Constantine to maintain the vision he was given by the Christian God, as well as keep his authority and influence upon all the organizations and activities, there had to be some compromise. In such matters as these, what will be compromised? It is simple—the environment.

This is when the first organized church came into being. Buildings were built for such an occasion. This allowed control over the religious activities of the masses. But, what would you do with the idolatrous or pagan ways of those who had power and influence? You simply cover them up with what would appear as religious rituals or activities, while advocating Christian tenets of faith. Although Christianity is about change occurring within, in this type of environment, a person could comply outwardly while maintaining their former idols and pagan practices. Perhaps some

---

[6] 2 Kings 17:4-33

would even get "good saved," but, nevertheless, there was compromise occurring.

The stronger Christians, no doubt, maintained their level of sincere worship, but there was a mixture developing. There were people who were pagan inwardly with their idols that simply took the God of Christianity and instituted Him into their idolatrous and pagan ways. Sadly, the term "Christian" was also being attached to these practices to keep everyone happy. The problem with attaching the term "Christian" to an idolatrous or pagan way is that it will eventually begin to desensitize or spiritually dull God's people to what is holy and what is profane.

We can clearly see this taking place in America. The term, "Christian" has been hijacked by many religions. The reason for this is because there is no clarity or distinction as to what really constitutes genuine Christianity. The visible Church is so full of the world that it has lost its edge and distinct identity.

As a result, people perceive if you are religious, somewhat moral, and a freedom-loving patriot, that you are a Christian. The truth is such individuals will possess an unholy mixture that may appear religious and decent according to the world, but the only identifying factor of the Christian life is missing. This point of identification is the divine presence and life of Jesus Christ.

When you bring the holy and unholy together, you will compromise the spirit that is in operation in the environment. Most people do not realize that there is a spirit in operation in the world, the church, and the home. This is why *1 John 4:1* instructs us to test the spirits.

We know that the spirit of the world works disobedience in those who are motivated by it. This spirit is not only clearly in operation in the world, but it is very prevalent in many homes as man often operates according to the independence of his own natural spirit. However, for the religious scene, it is the antichrist spirit that operates from a fleshly and worldly platform. This spirit is very religious, but its main work is to become a substitute for the real Jesus by replacing Him with dead religion, worldly and heretical beliefs, and lifeless activities.[7]

The Bible is clear that God has not given us the spirit of the world. He not only gives born-again believers a new heart, but He also gives them His Spirit. The Holy Spirit will have no part in any belief or practice where there is a mixture of the holy with the unholy. He will not move on or in such an environment.

The Spirit of God is within the believer, but He is also the connection between the Head who is sitting on the right hand of God and the Body of believers. In other words, He not only moves within the believer, but He must move upon the believer and the Body as the rivers of Living Water from the throne of God. This is how the Holy Spirit ensures His presence in the midst of His people. He does this for the purpose of building the Body up into the Head. It is through this connection with the throne of God that He fills or refreshes the believer and the Body, as well as brings forth wisdom and revelation.[8]

If the Holy Spirit encounters any compromise or unholy agreement within the environment, He will immediately be quenched. For the Spirit to be quenched means there is no point of communion or edification in which the members of the Church can get their spiritual bearings and come into real fellowship together.

The Spirit will end up being grieved by the sin of unbelief that will begin to operate in such an atmosphere, as man-influenced beliefs, rituals, experiences, or practices begin to replace the validity of the Word. As a result, He will depart and, since the Holy Spirit is the source of life in the Body of Christ, the heavenly

---

[7] Proverbs 25:27-28; Ephesians 2:2; 4:13-16; Colossians 2:2-8; 1 John 4:1

[8] Genesis 1:2; John 7:37-39; 16:13; 1 Corinthians 3:12; Ephesians 1:17; 3:3-5;   4:15-16; 5:18

connection and power from above will subtly evaporate out of the environment, leaving a spiritual vacuum.[9]

For those who are truly Christians, this type of environment will eventually cause restlessness in their souls. They sense something is missing, but they cannot always figure out what is absent. Perhaps Christ is being preached, and the buildings might be full of people that never before named the name of Christ. Perhaps there are many religious activities going on, making it all seem quite successful. However, something is missing.

What is missing is the Holy Spirit. According to *Isaiah 30:1*, He is to serve as our only covering. However, such unholy compromises will bring people under a wicked covering that will prevent the heavenly connection from ever being made. In fact, this covering or veil will blind people to the real Gospel.[10]

Now that the Spirit is missing, what will replace Him and His work in the Church? It is important that we realize every vacant environment or spot in our lives must be filled with something.[11] As you will discover in the next chapter, such an environment places the members of the Body of Christ in a precarious position. It is a position that will not only cause restlessness in the spirit, but will bring them to a dangerous crossroads in which a decision will be required.

---

[9] 1 Samuel 16:14; Romans 10:17; 2 Corinthians 13:14; Ephesians 4:30; 1 Thessalonians 5:19
[10] Isaiah 25:7; 2 Corinthians 4:3-6
[11] Matthew 12:43-45

4

THE REPLACEMENT

What happens when the Holy Spirit is missing from the environment? Once again, we must be reminded that environments influence our attitudes toward God and life. Our attitudes will determine what we expose ourselves to, as well as the agendas and values we develop along the way.

As you consider Christianity, you must realize that it is a way of life that is meant to influence every aspect of our mindsets, attitudes, agendas, and priorities. As a result, it will determine our approach to matters and our conduct in regard to our different responsibilities.

It is vital that we have the connection of heaven, the Holy Spirit, moving within us and upon us. He is the one who informs us of the matters of heaven through wisdom, knowledge, and revelation. He will warn us of things to come in order to prepare us for future events. To ensure and adhere to this connection of heaven means that we must follow after the Spirit in order to do what is right before God. We must be led by the Spirit in order to do what is honorable and reasonable in our Christian conduct, and we must walk in the Spirit to ensure that we are within the will of God in all matters of devotion and service.[1]

When the Holy Spirit is missing from the environment, a believer could basically find themself in what could be considered

---

[1] John 16:13; Ephesians 1:17; 3:3-5; Colossians 2:3; Romans 8:1, 13-14; Galatians 5:16

a comfort zone. In this zone, there is nothing that is clearly right or wrong, but there is also nothing really happening in the spiritual realm.

As one considers such an environment, there is no real detection that there is something blatantly wrong in one's lifestyle or relationship with God. In fact, the Christian appearance is still intact. However, such a state is referred to as lukewarm.

According to the Bible, this is a very dangerous state to be in. There will be no sharpness in which discernment is maintained, fine-tuned, or developed. Without discernment, a believer will not be aware of what is really going on in their environment. Without the sharpness of discernment, Christians can actually come into agreement with the unholy without any sense that a terrible error has been made.[2]

The other problem is that it is a natural tendency for the selfish disposition of the old man to rise up its head and subtly gain preeminence in such a state, bringing the person under the influence of the spirit of the world. Without discernment, a believer will not even be aware that they are sliding into a slime pit of their old ways. This is why the Apostle Paul admonished those who are asleep to awake from the influences of darkness upon their lives.[3]

An environment in which the Spirit is missing can be related to the popular example of a pot of water with a frog in it. Of course, in the compromising state of complacency, the believer is the frog. The fire is turned on under the pot, but it is done in such a way that it is slowly being brought to a boil. Since the frog is initially adjusting to the change, it is unaware of the precarious position it is in.

Sadly, the unholy compromise that took place in the fourth century between the man's version of religion and the Church put the Church in a pot of water. Without knowing it, the fire of

---

[2] 1 Corinthians 2:9-14; Revelation 3:14-18
[3] Ephesians 5:14-17

influence and compromise has been slowly turned up, taking away the discernment and life of the professing Church. It is now important to identify this pot of water. In fact, as you study the big struggle between the professing Church and the watchmen, you will see that this is a common denominator that is brought out in their warnings. The pot is the world.

Any time you add the unholy (the ways and philosophies of the world) to the holy (the ways of God), the end result will be carnal or fleshly. It may be a comfortable compromise for those who are trying to live in peace with the different aspects of the world, but, as believers in the Body of Christ, the real edge has been compromised. That edge is the presence, power, and working of the Spirit. Instead of being distinct, the believer or Church is now giving up their connection to the Head to come under the spirit of the world in the name of compromise, tolerance, and self-preservation.[4]

In his book *You Will Receive Power*, William Law stated that the real sin of all sins, or the heresy of all heresies comes down to the influence and power of the worldly spirit. It is not unusual to minimize the agreement or power the spirit of the world has even had on believers, but as Law pointed out in his book, it is the great apostasy from God and the life He wants to bring forth in and through His saints. The spirit of the world is not simply a sin that finds its basis in unbelief or idolatry; rather, it represents the essence of the disposition of sin that works in us. Every sin is a branch that finds its source in or influenced by the spirit of the world.[5]

The spirit of the world causes us to replace the best or the excellent goodness and ways of God with what seems right, acceptable, and nominal to the world. However, as Law pointed out, to depart one degree from God's goodness means you are

---

[4] 2 Corinthians 6:14-18; Ephesians 2:2; James 4:4
[5] pg. 137

departing into evil. To choose or embrace any other life but that which comes from God is to choose the ways of death.[6]

The spirit of the world will call for reformation to the self-life, but the Holy Spirit requires us to deny the self-life. The world offers the self-life happiness, but the Spirit and the Word of God reveals that the self-life is void of being satisfied and must be put down in order to discover real life. As Law pointed out in his book, the self-life is the whole essence of our fallen disposition, but denial of self is our capacity to be saved while humility is our savior.[7]

Surely, the Christians of the fourth century had no intention of giving up their edge, but the reality is that the spirit of the world came into the midst of the professing Church. From the basis of this unholy compromise, the world began to influence the mind of the professing Church with each subtle compromise of its idolatrous or pagan beliefs or philosophies.[8]

As the environment of the professing Church changed, the worldview of it began to change as well. In other words, the world was now influencing how the visible Church would view the world around it. The lines between good and evil became blurred.

It is important to point out that every leader of the new Church struggled with this very issue. The Head of the Body, Jesus, warned that, since the world hated Him, it would hate those who are His followers. He than gave this warning in *Luke 6:26, "Woe unto you, when all men shall speak well of you! For so did their father to the false prophets."*

There are those in the professing Church who believe they must keep peace with the world. However, such compromise will bring them into a state of utter sorrow, despair, and judgment. After all, the world will truly hate those who are followers of Jesus

---

[6] Ibid
[7] Ibid, pg. 80
[8] Colossians 2:8

because they do not belong to the world, nor will they have any part in it.[9]

When you consider the writings of the New Testament, it is full of admonishment to believers to come out and be separate from the world. James told us that those who love the world are spiritual harlots, and they will find themselves considered enemies of God. The Apostle John warned us the world will pass away, but those who do the will of God will live forever. The Apostle Paul instructed believers to come out and be separate from that which is contrary to the Spirit of God and the leadership of Christ. After all, there can be no such agreement between the Christian and the pagan ways of the world's idolatry, philosophies, and perverted practices.[10]

Finally, there is the soulful reality that some believers not only fail to consecrate themselves totally to God, but they go back to their former lives that they had in the world. We have the examples of the disciples who were offended by the truth, and, from that time on, they went back and walked no more with Jesus. There was also a man by the name of Demas. He was part of the Apostle Paul's ministry team. His name is recorded in Paul's letters.[11] However, the apostle made this mention of him in his last letter, *"For Demas hath forsaken me, having loved this present world, and is departed unto Thessalonica..." (2 Timothy 4:10a).*

The world is very alluring when it comes to the self-life, with all of its fleshly appetites. This is the platform the world uses to gain our dependency upon it. It knows how to attract our pride to gain our loyalty and support. Its clever propaganda is designed to convince us that it is the real source of our hope in finding happiness and purpose. The world's false glory gains the attention of our eyes so we will pursue its deceptive beauty, rather than the

---

[9] John 7:7; 17:14-16
[10] 2 Corinthians 6:14-18; James 4:4; 1 John 2:15-17
[11] John 6:66; Colossians 4:14; Philemon 24

glories of heaven. As we become entangled in its destructive web, we begin to discover that its seductive ways only lead to emptiness and bondage and that its attractions result in a freefall into utter despair and defeat. The propaganda of the world leaves us depressed and skeptical, while its beauty becomes bitterness to the soul.

The reality of the world is that it has no life to offer. It has a façade, or semblance of life and false promises in regard to an idea or image of life, but there is no real life in any of it. In fact, behind this idea of life, is a vacuum that proves to be dark and hollow. For this reason, the Apostle Paul stated that he was crucified to the world, and it was crucified to him. Obviously, the world had no more power to influence or attract him into its destructive web.[12]

The Apostle Paul's attitude towards the world was the result of him being realistic about the value and worth of the world. He actually counted his activities associated to the flesh, his earthly heritage as a Jew, and his misdirected devotion to the Law as dung. He realized all temporary pleasure, honor, and sacrifice was a complete loss in light of gaining the very treasure of heaven, Jesus Christ.[13] Paul's attitude reminds us of the challenge put forth by Jesus to all of His followers, *"For what is a man profited, if he shall gain the whole world, and lose his own soul? Or what shall a man give in exchange for his soul?" (Matthew 16:26).*

What is your soul worth to you? What is my soul worth to me? God estimated the cost of our souls and gave His only begotten Son in our place on the cross. Jesus estimated the cost of our souls and offered up His life on our behalf. But we must also personally estimate the worth of our souls. If we value the world, we will sacrifice our souls to possess what is temporary and what already stands judged. On the other hand, the cost to possess our

---

[12] Galatians 6:14
[13] Philippians 3:4-8

souls for the purpose of presenting our bodies as a living sacrifice, consecrated for the use, purpose, and glory of God will ultimately cost us our identification, agreement, and association with the world. We cannot possess the life of Christ and be in agreement with the spirit of the world at the same time. What is ultimately offered up will be based on the estimation we put on our own personal souls and ideas of life.

The struggle for saints to come out and be separate from the world is not new to God's people. We can see this same struggle in Israel's case. Egypt represented the world to the people of Israel. In the beginning, their presence as a foreign entity in Egypt seemed harmless. As time went on, these foreign people became a threat to Egypt. To control them, they were brought into bondage. The bondage made them slaves to a cruel taskmaster, and, as a result, they began to cry out to God in their oppression.[14]

God sent a deliverer by the name of Moses. Moses had to lead the children of Israel away from Egypt. But, before he could accomplish such a feat, all of the Egyptian's idols had to be humbled before the children of Israel. This was to show them that Jehovah God was the one and only true God of heaven and earth.

Clearly, God had to get a hold of the people's minds so that they could see the contrast between the lifeless idols and empty, pagan practices of the age they lived in to embrace the One who was and is the great I AM.[15] As the great I AM, God was and is the ever-present reality of the past, the present, and the future about the matters of life and death. The great "I AM" points to God as the essence of all wisdom, as He brings the lessons of the past into the present to change the outcome of the future.

The children of Israel had to be totally separated from the influences of Egypt for God to influence their minds and hearts. Behind such influence was the wisdom of the ages. This wisdom's

---

[14] Exodus 1:8-14; 2:23-25
[15] Exodus 3:14-15

main thrust was and always will be to bring forth God's promises and plan through His people. Since the people of Israel had been chosen out of the world, they needed to become a separate, holy people, consecrated unto Jehovah God for His work and glory.

Although the children of Israel came out of their present world, it did not come out of them. They brought the world with them. In other words, their affections were still tied to the world they had known. This is why they were quick to resort to pagan attitudes and practices when they worshipped the golden calf and complained about the manna that fell short of the variety of tastes they had experienced in Egypt.

Sadly, because of their affections that remained with their former existence, they never really developed reliance upon Jehovah God. Their submission to their former way of thinking resulted in judgment falling upon the generation of adults who came out of Egypt. The "old" generation would not enter the Promised Land, and the generation that finally entered the place God had promised to Abraham had no memories of Egypt, or the memories had been dimmed by their years in the wilderness.[16]

The world ceased to be a temptation to the children of Israel. As a result, they could embrace the blessings of God. However, the children of Israel were about to embark into the midst of the alluring seductions of the idols of the present world or age, along with their various unholy practices. Since the children of Israel were born into the Adamic race, these seductions would prove to be effective temptations to their carnal affections and youthful lusts.

God warned the people of Israel about coming into agreement with any aspect of the world. They were told to rid the land of the people that adhered to such profane worship and practices. Most

---

[16] If you are interested in the spiritual lessons the children of Israel's examples teach believers, see the author's book, *The Victorious Journey*.

of us should know the rest of the story. The children of Israel became slack in their responsibility to rid the land of any possible temptation or unholy agreement. As a result, they opened a door to the world, and the world came into their midst through the idols and pagan practices of the heathen people. Consider what was said about this open door,

> *Know for a certainty that the LORD your God will no more drive out any of these nations from before you; but they shall be snares and traps unto you, and scourges in your sides, and thorns in your eyes, until you perish from off this good land which the LORD your God hath given (Joshua 23:13).*

When you consider what is being said here, this open door to the world doomed the kingdom of Israel. It would take hundreds of years before Israel would come down in judgment because of its unholy agreements, but it would spend hundreds of years more in subjection to the heavy yokes and hatred of the world.

The world stands condemned. Therefore, everything that comes into agreement with it, is associated with it, or looks to it is condemned as well. At first, a relationship with the world may seem harmless enough, but it will slowly ensnare a person into its entanglements and trap them into its lies. Once a person is entrapped, the world will turn around to scourge a person for foolishly falling into its traps of deception, as well as blind them to the despair and depression that is engulfing their soul.

A good example of the destruction of the world is Lot's wife. She was taken out of the world (Sodom and Gomorrah) because of her association to Lot, who was vexed by the cities' spiritual condition. However, her affections were still loyal to the world. She looked back at it as it was being judged and turned into a pillar of salt.[17] Hence enters a very important warning from Jesus in regard to following Him into a service of devotion and worship, "*No man,*

---

[17] Genesis 19:1-29; 2 Peter 2:6-8

having put his hand to the plough (to follow me), and looking back (to the world), is fit for the kingdom of God" (Luke 9:62b, parentheses added).

Every Christian is called to be completely separate from the world, but few choose to do so. As a result, few are chosen to enter into all that God has made available to His people. Clearly, Christians must choose to completely close that door to the world, which represents their former life. They must recognize that Jesus came to redeem their souls, but the world desires to enslave and destroy their souls. Therefore, they must choose whom they will serve, the God of heaven or the idols of this present world. They must decide who or what will influence their minds, the wisdom of heaven or the foolishness of this present age. They must decide who will claim the loyalty of their affections, the Head of the Church, Jesus Christ, or the god of this present world, Satan.[18]

Every day, Christians must deny self, neglect pride, hate evil, pick up their crosses, and follow Jesus. The world must not only be considered dung to believers, but dead, a vacant tomb of utter destruction that is void of any real hope of life.

What about you? What is your attitude toward the world? Has the door of its influence been completely shut down or is it still defining your life and values?

---

[18] Matthew 6:24

Part II

THE SHIFT
FROM CENTER

5

THE OPEN DOOR

In the fourth century of the new Church, a door was opened that started the professing Church down a precarious path. The door that was opened was to the influences of the world. This allowed the spirit of the world to come into the midst of the Church.

As you follow the first three centuries of the Church, the message was consistent: "Come out from the world and be separate." One of the individuals who contended for the faith of the Christians in the second century was a man named Tertullian.

He was born around A.D. 150. Even though Tertullian was fluent in Greek, he wrote most of his works in Latin in order to benefit the growing number of western Christians who only spoke Latin. He often developed Latin terminology to express truths that had been primarily presented in the Greek language. One of the most famous Latin terms that he coined to express the Godhead was the word "trinity."[1]

In Tertullian's writings, the world's influence upon the believers was one of the foremost issues he confronted. Many of the Christians were coming out from under, or were still struggling with the strong influence of the Roman Empire. As you consider the rulers of Rome, you see that they emphasized greater entertainment for the masses in order to keep them happy and win

---

[1] A Glimpse at Early Christian Life; Tertullian, © 1991 by David W. Bercot, pgs. 1-2

their favor. As a result, people gladly sold their votes, as well as their souls to taste the many idolatrous and pagan flavors of this decadent society. One of those flavors included watching Christians' blood spilled in the Roman arenas in the name of sensational entertainment.

On top of the entertainment was the extravagance of dress and food. Every tempting taste was presented, while the eyes of the people were being enlarged by the covetousness of the surrounding environment. Although the affairs of Rome sometimes challenged these people's unrealistic world of sensationalism, they always had a fix waiting for them around the corner or in the coliseums, where they watched and cheered for their latest hero as he faced death in the name of entertainment. Does this sound familiar?

If you conduct a serious, comparative study of the environment of Rome and the present environment of America, there is basically no difference. Granted, we Americans are a bit more "civilized" about the type of entertainment we will allow, but the same environment exists today. History is simply repeating itself. Like Rome, America's societies are doomed by her own worldly, idolatrous, gluttonous, immoral, and decadent ways.

Meanwhile every true watchman of God will sound the same alarm. The door has been opened wide to the world, the gate of discernment has been let down in the Church, and now the enemy is not only in our midst, but is trying to invade every arena of our lives.

It is important to understand that, when a Christian is saved, they are given a new heart or disposition, but they still have the same tendencies. These tendencies are based on worldly mindsets and practices. As a result, the mind must be transformed in order to change the attitude.[2] Once the attitude is changed

---

[2] Ezekiel 36:26-27; Romans 12:2; Hebrews 10:15-17

towards the world's influences, the tendencies or habits will also change.

As Christians, we must understand that being saved places us above the world in heavenly places with Christ. But the world is not completely out of us. Because of our initial premise of being a Christian, which is fleshly, we only can know in part. We also see in part because we are still looking through the "glass" of the world.[3]

The world includes such influences as religion, culture, worldly relationships, philosophies, and practices. Therefore, much of our understanding is based on what we have been exposed to or have experienced in our flesh. It is from this worldly understanding or view that we naturally interpret what we see or encounter, including our spiritual understanding and experiences.

Since the world initially has a hold of our minds, it will own the lusts, appetites, or desires of our affections. As Christians, we must claim them back and redirect them in the right direction. To change such a perspective is not something that happens overnight. We must constantly discipline our thoughts and affections.[4] In fact, we must do an incredible juggling act between the two opposing kingdoms of darkness and light, which requires integrity and meekness on our part.

As Jesus' Body, we Christians will remain in this world, but we must cease to be part of it, for any agreement with it is spiritual fornication. Remember the temptations that caused us to fall in the past are still present in the world we live in. Due to our tendencies to justify sin and satisfy our fleshly appetites, it is easy to give way to any old or new temptations that may come our way. This is why the Apostle Paul stated he counted all associations with the world as dung, and he became crucified to the world, and the world to him. He also stressed that he died daily and brought

---

[3] Ephesians 2:6; 1 Corinthians 13:9, 12
[4] 2 Corinthians 10:3-5; Colossians 3:1-2

his body into subjection so that he would not be a castaway or reprobate in the end.[5]

Clearly, Paul understood that the world remained his enemy, even in his consecrated life before God. He had to maintain a right attitude at all times towards the world, as well as guard his affections and discipline his involvement and activities. James summarized the struggle in this manner, *"But every man is tempted, when he is drawn away of his own lust, and enticed. Then when lust hath conceived, it bringeth forth sin; and sin, when it is finished, bringeth forth death" (James 1:14-15).*

By the world being in the midst of the vulnerable Church, it now had the means to, once again, ensnare the Lord's sheep into its destructive web. The ways of the world are cleverly designed to appear as a Christian's solution when the person's spiritual guard is down.

Although the world's attractions and ways are nothing more than a fanciful deception, it begins to wear down a person's resolve to maintain a spiritual and emotional discernment, as well as a physical separation. As the person becomes more enticed by the possibilities of how the world is able to become their solution, it begins to rob the person of discernment. Eventually, with enough enticement, it can kill a person's ability to discern its influence, ultimately destroying any remaining resolve to stand against it.

In the end, the practices of the world will not seem evil to this individual, but logical. The attitude that was once firmly set against it will begin to adjust as it begins to see consecration as fanaticism, rather than one's reasonable service. Once the attitude is changed, it will mock any stand for truth and holiness that will not bend with the changing winds of the world that are allowed to blow through Christendom without any warning or instruction.

[5] 1 Corinthians 6:13-16; 9:27; 15:31; 2 Corinthians 10:3-5; Philippians 3:4-8; Colossians 3:1-2

It is clear that, as Christians, our initial attitude towards the world must be totally changed so we can unlearn the idolatrous ways and pagan practices of it. Often, unbeknown to us, these practices still have the power to influence our mindsets, attitudes, and tendencies.

To unlearn the ways of the world means to change the value and importance it holds in our lives. To change our value system, we must expose ourselves to and learn the perfect and holy ways of God. Learning who God is will establish a proper attitude towards Him. However, this means getting into the Word of God in order for it to get into us to cleanse and transform the way we look at the world around us. We must seek godly fellowship, flee those things that appeal to youthful lust, and separate ourselves from the vain activities of the world, while pursuing what is righteous.[6]

This brings us back to what happened to the Church. The godly shepherds and watchmen of the Church were forever calling the sheep to come out of the world and be completely separate from all of its influence upon their minds and affections. This was the only way new believers would unlearn the ways of the world in order to implement the righteous ways of God in their attitudes and practices. There had to be an exchange. By separating from the world and unlearning its wicked ways, a person would have the liberty to separate unto God in total consecration.

By Christians separating from the world and unlearning its wicked ways to embrace the life of Jesus, they could develop an excellent spirit like Daniel possessed when he was in Babylon. Babylon was also idolatrous and decadent. However, Daniel had purposed in his heart to be upright before Jehovah God.[7] This allowed him to maintain His life in God in the midst of the idolatrous and unholy. He never came into agreement with it or

---

[6] Deuteronomy 4:10; 18:9; 2 Timothy 2:15-16, 21-26
[7] Daniel 1:8; 6:3

submitted to the temptation as a means to keep peace with it. Jehovah God was his God and Lord, and he refused to compromise any of his relationship or life in God as a means to "get along" with the present age.

Daniel is one of the many examples in the Word of God that teaches us how to be in the world without becoming part of it. This is the main struggle between the Spirit and the flesh.[8] As Christians, we must not only find Christ in the midst of this confusing mess, but we must maintain a complete separation from it as a means to maintain our spiritual edge and witness in the midst of the world's great darkness.

The fourth-century Church had unknowingly opened the door to the world, which was now subtly coming into the midst of the believers. The Church had not come into agreement with the spirit of the world, but the gate of truth and discernment would be eventually let down, ultimately changing the face of the visible, professing Church.

Once the door to the world opened, the Holy Spirit lifted from such an environment, leaving a vacuum that would be filled by the spirit of the world with its many different influences. How would the world's influences upon the professing Church express itself?

The world operates according to systems. These systems organize people according to agenda, purpose, and vision. Since the world operates according to systems, it would not be hard for it to organize religion into a nice controllable box. Although the world operates according to systems, it is men's influences based upon worldly philosophies and practices within those systems that will determine how people will be organized.

Needless to say, the operations of this system will look very religious. It will claim its authority and rights according to its association with God and His Word. It will also advocate morality in action and goodness towards the brotherhood. However, since

---

[8] Galatians 5:16-17

it is carnal and not spiritual, it will appeal to the emotions, pride, and decency of people. Such appeal will express itself in good works, but it will lack true spirit and life, making it a counterfeit of true Christianity.

Once the Holy Spirit is missing, man will step into the Spirit's place to serve as a conscience and interpreter of God's Word. It is important to point out that a religious system was very much in operation in Jesus' day. There had been a period of 400 years of silence (meaning there were no direct revelations from God through prophets) between the Old and New Testaments. The voice of God had once again been silenced due to sin and idolatry among His people.

When you study the history of the Jewish people, you can see the traumatic crisis that their faith suffered. There was one upheaval after another in the political and religious realms. In the midst of these constant struggles, a weaker group known as the Pharisees strived to tenaciously hold on to the Jewish Law, although they added various nonessential traditions to it. The name "Pharisee" was taken from a root word meaning "to separate".

On the other hand, there was another faction that added contemporary Grecian ways and customs to religious attitudes and practices. These particular Jews saw no real deliverance for Israel; therefore, they decided to make a covenant with the heathen. They sought out different ways in which to popularize their practices to make them acceptable to both worlds. These individuals became predecessors of the polished, but infidel, Sadducees.[9]

These two groups give us an insight into what happens when the Spirit of God is missing from the equation. The end result is two extremes that operate according to two distinct philosophies.

---

[9] The Four Hundred Silent Years; H. A. Ironside; 16th printing 1980; Loizeaux Brothers, Inc. pgs. 32-33

In fact, the two great systems that were vying for the minds of the people during Paul's day were Stoicism and Epicureanism.

The philosophy behind Stoicism is to live nobly and death will not matter. The philosophy behind Epicureanism is that all is uncertain, so, therefore, enjoy life to the fullness regardless of the moral implications.[10] Whether we want to admit it or not, most religions that are inspired by those who belong to this present world will fall under the attitude of one or the other of these philosophies.

The fruits easily identified the influences of these two worldly philosophies upon the minds of people. For example, since the Spirit was missing and not inspiring the Pharisees according to the life of God, they held the truth in carnal or fleshly ways. These were, and are, the people who adjust the ways of God to their self-righteous conclusions, while neglecting the spiritual aspect or intent of God's ways. These people prove to be judgmental.

The other group came into blatant agreement with the world. Their pursuit was according to the popularity of the world. We know that the Sadducees denied even the doctrine of the resurrection from the dead.[11]

There was also a third party that was present during Jesus' day. They were feeble and afflicted. They abhorred the ways of the heathen, while refusing to give way to the legal pretensions of those who were self-righteous and legalistic. They clung to God's Word and the promise of the coming Messiah. They became eventually known as the Essenes.[12] *Smith's Bible Dictionary* describes these three groups by referring to the Pharisees as Formalists, the Sadducees as the Freethinkers, and the Essenes as the Puritans.

---

[10] Lectures on Colossians; H. A. Ironside; 15TH printing, May 1978; Published by Loizeaux Brothers, Inc. pg. 73

[11] Matthew 22:23-33; Hebrews 6:1-2

[12] The Four Hundred Silent Years; pg. 33

In the midst of the struggle to maintain the purity of the Jewish faith during these four hundred years of silence between the Old and New Testaments, a few men of the priesthood, with the last name of Maccabeus, defied the worldly powers to be such as Antiochus. This started a revolution that cost many of the Jews their very lives because they openly refused to submit to the idolatrous ways being thrust upon them from those who were considered uncircumcised.[13]

However, this conflict went on for years, and even developed within the priesthood. Sadly, the door to the world was again opened when one of the religious leaders made a pact with the Roman Empire to bring some semblance of peace to the conflict that raged within the leadership of the Jewish priesthood. Once again, the people of God began to lose their edge due to the reality that the Spirit would not have any part in such an agreement.

When Jesus entered the worldly scene, the Pharisees and Sadducees were forces to be reckoned with. Although two distinct sects, they had influence in the political realm. When you consider Pilate, Jesus was offered as a peace offering to keep a semblance of peace with the religious leadership of the Jewish religion.

Compromising with that which is contrary to maintain some semblance of peace is a pattern that can be easily followed. However, it ultimately leads to destruction. We see this in the case of the end days, as many will come under the destructive rule of an anti-Christ reign in the name of peace. This fragile peace will disrupt into utter chaos, death, and ruin.

To answer the question that was posed earlier in this chapter, how would the system of the world express itself through religion? It will express itself through carnality that does not properly handle the truth, or it will use the agreement with the world to promote its religious causes.

---

[13] Ibid, pgs. 46-47

Can we not see this same state of affairs in today's professing Church? We either see the philosophy of harsh legalism that has no life in it, or we see the liberal philosophies and methods of the world being instituted into Christians' beliefs and practices. Whether we arrogantly refer to one extreme as being conservative and the other as being liberal, the Spirit is missing from both types of systems or philosophies. If the Spirit of God is not present, such religious attitudes and practices must be regarded as carnal.

Carnality is nothing more than man's best attempts to make himself acceptable to God. Such attempts are worldly in nature, but they have proven to be a successful means by which to clothe the world in some righteous garb and sell it as a bill of goods to the professing Church.

What does Scripture say about all of this? *Isaiah 64:6* tells us that man's best is considered filthy rags to God. The Apostle Paul stated that the wrath of God will be revealed from heaven against those who hold the truth in any type of ungodliness and unrighteousness.

We are also reminded that Jesus did not come to reconcile the systems of the world to Himself, but lost man. The world is already condemned, along with those who love and serve it. We also have Jesus' warning that it does not matter what great acts one might do in His name; if they are not according to the will of the Father, they will be considered iniquity.[14]

As you consider the history of God's people, you will realize that the greater the influence of the world upon their minds and hearts, the further away they slid from the center of that which was and remains to be true, pure, and holy. We know the center is God, and, when God is not our reality as believers, we become lost in the emptiness of religious acts and the ridiculousness of man's rules and conclusions.

---

[14] Matthew 7:21-23; Romans 1:18; Ephesians 2:13-18

What about you? Do you sense that much that goes on in Christendom is foolish and void of substance? If you answer yes to these two questions, then you need to know you are not alone. But you also must realize that it is up to each believer individually to come back to center, regardless of the environment, to develop an excellent spirit before God.

6

THE SHIFT
IN LEADERSHIP

The world can only organize activities according to its systems. When the world came into the midst of the Church, man began to organize religion. Buildings were built to set up the environment that would control the activities of the professing Church. Leadership had to be defined in order to maintain the control or order that was being put forth. Practices were instituted to cause an appearance of righteous activities. Most of these practices were idolatrous and pagan. However, they were being repackaged and presented in the light of Christian titles and so-called "responsibilities".

When you follow the progression of the world's influence upon the Church, you can clearly see how everything in the true Church was redefined to fit the world's agendas and presentation. Let's face it; the world has been clearly trying to define the Church for centuries, rather than the Body of Christ being defined by the Head (Christ) and Spirit of God. As a result, the face of the visible Church has changed.

It is vital that we follow this progression to understand how Christians now possess a misconception about the real Church of Jesus Christ. The primitive Church was not visible due to persecution. The members did not always have set places where they came together in one accord. They had no recorded membership, other than that their names were written in the Book of Life. They did not stand out in the world as the greatest or most successful religion the world had ever seen; rather, they were to stand apart from the world in their hearts, mindsets, and lifestyle. It would be this distinction, not necessarily verbal claims, which would draw people to Jesus Christ. In such drawing, the simple Gospel would be shared and preached under the anointing, authority, and power of the Spirit.

The new Church had typical struggles. However, the members were clear about their commission and responsibility in light of the world. Their commission was to preach the Gospel and make disciples of Jesus. Their religious responsibility was to remain distinct from the world so that they could maintain their edge, authority, and power.

This edge, authority, and power were necessary for them to fulfill their high calling in Christ Jesus in devotion, worship, and service.[1] Although the Church had practices that were clearly ordained in Scripture, its responsibility would also be clear. The members had to keep such practices from losing the simplicity of meaning and the inspirational power and life of the Spirit.

Sadly, man is a creature of habit due to the persuasion of his fleshly disposition and the persuasion of the world; therefore, he is not inclined or disciplined to maintain the connection to heaven. Because of this tendency, practices, such as communion, baptism, and the laying on of hands, were often reduced to lifeless rituals and ceremonies that lost their impact upon hearts and minds.[2]

Since the world came into the midst of the Church, the leadership had to be defined. Up until this point, the leadership of the Church was clearly in place. Jesus was to be the Head of the

---

[1] James 1:27

[2] Deeper Experiences of Famous Christians; James Gilchrist Lawson, © 2000 by Barbour Publishing, Inc. pg. 50

Body, the Spirit of God was to serve as the covering, and the Word was to serve as the Body's final authority in all manners of truth, righteousness, doctrine, and practices.[3]

There were positions stipulated for the purpose of establishing the Body upon the foundation of Jesus according to the Father's design. However, these positions were to be marked by humility before God, as well as submission and servitude to others. In fact, God never called His servants to greater leadership, but to greater servitude. Such leadership would be contrary to the world's idea of greatness. Jesus clearly brought this out to His disciples in *Matthew 20:20-28.*

These positions of service included apostles, prophets, evangelists, pastors, and teachers.[4] Apostles were sent forth to establish local bodies of believers upon the Person of Jesus Christ. The prophets had the responsibility to guard the spiritual condition of the Body against falsehood. Such individuals would contend for the faith that was first delivered to the saints. The evangelists were to challenge the vision of the Body to ensure that the same fire that inspired the new believers on Pentecost remained alive with the flame of authority, power, and life of the heavenly and the eternal.

Pastors were also to serve as elders in the Body and were to oversee the welfare and maturity of God's sheep. Teachers were to challenge the minds and understanding of these sheep as they partook of the manna from heaven. Such manna would not only become life to the saints, but also strength and confidence that would enable them to embrace the impossible, as well as dare to discover the depths of God's incredible character and truths.

On the local level, the positions of elder (pastor and bishop) and deacon (minister) were set apart to establish, guard, and serve the local bodies. The elder was to impart the Word of God

---

[3] 2 Timothy 3:16-17
[4] Ephesians 4:11-12

to the sheep. The deacon was to be a servant of the needs of those in the local body, as well as to lift the burdens of ministry from the elders. This allowed the elders to commit themselves to preparation of properly dividing and imparting the truth to God's fold. These servants had to have impeccable character. After all, they were to serve as an extension of Jesus to His flock in example and service.[5]

Needless to say, the leadership of the Church has always been affronted in some way by the religious influences of man and the world. In John's revelation concerning the seven churches of Asia Minor, the Lord made strong statements concerning the deeds and doctrine of the Nicolaitanes. He even told the local bodies of Ephesus and Pergamum that He held hatred towards their activities and influence.[6] But, who were the Nicolaitanes, and what deeds and doctrine were they purporting?

As Christians, we must understand what is always under attack when it comes to the spiritual foundation of our lives. It is easy to think that certain belief systems or doctrines (teachings) are what come under attack. The simple reality is that popular and accepted beliefs may be challenged, and there may be attempts to twist fundamental doctrines to fit personal agendas, but what comes under attack is the integrity of God's truth.

Jesus, who is our foundation, serves as the essence of all absolute truth regarding God, the Gospel, and eternal life. However, His truth has no power in the lives of people unless it is unadulterated, and the Spirit is the One who firmly leads believers into understanding the intent of such truth in their lives. This is why the Apostle Paul exhorted believers to love the truth, ensuring the salvation of their very souls.[7]

---

[5] Acts 6:2-7; 1 Timothy 3:2-13; Titus 1:5-14
[6] Revelation 2:6, 15
[7] John 14:6; 1 Corinthians 3:11; 2 Thessalonians 2:10

It is vital that we, as believers, understand the battle that was raging in the midst of these different local bodies in the book of Revelation. We also must keep in mind what happened to the light of the testimony or witness of these seven churches. They have all ceased to burn. In fact, the Muslin faith now claims preeminence where these different local bodies once served as living witnesses in their dark age.

As we consider the Nicolaitanes, we must come to an understanding of whether they represented some religious sect, or if they were a movement on the part of a certain group of people to bring about some type of mixture that had the flavor of Christianity, but was void of the life of Jesus and the Spirit of God. Since there is no indication that it was a sect from historical sources, we might conclude that it was some type of religious movement that was trying to take root in the Church.

Since we don't have much to go on except the few Scriptures that mentioned the Nicolaitanes, we need to consider the text in which they were discussed. The main key possibly rests with the likely meaning behind the name, the references, and the environments that were present. The environment will tell us the possible weakness in the Body that would make it susceptible to become indifferent and possibly influenced by this religious movement.

In *Revelation 2:6,* the Christians of Ephesus recognized the deeds of the Nicolaitanes. Deeds imply labor, work, or occupation.[8] In the case of Pergamos, there was a doctrine that was being taught. Doctrine has to do with teaching people what is required of them as far as their spiritual responsibilities and conduct in matters. A good example of Christian doctrine is the teachings concerning marriage in *Ephesians 5:22-33.* It is important to mention that doctrine is meant to influence conduct

---

[8] Strong's Exhaustive Concordance of the Bible; James Strong, © 1986 assigned to World Bible Publishers, Inc. #2041

in light of establishing a right attitude about something. Therefore, this teaching of the Nicolaitanes would not only determine conduct, but influence attitude towards spiritual truths.

The Body of Ephesus hated the deeds of the Nicolaitanes, while the Body of Pergamos allowed the Nicolaitanes in their midst. Clearly, the members of the Pergamos local body were not condemning and separating themselves from their teachings.

In his booklet on this subject, F. W. Grant points out that the Greek meaning of Nicolaitane is what will most likely give us a clue into what those promoting the movement might have been advocating. It means "conquering the people."

Apparently, the Greek word which was used for "the people" in this text and our commonly-used term "laity" is derived from the same word, "laos." In Grant's conclusion, this could mean only one thing—that the masses of people (laity) were being put down by those who were now being considered the special class of people, or what we would refer to as the clergy.[9]

As believers, we must immediately recognize that this separation is discarding the makeup and function of the true Body. Instead of having one Head over the Body, certain people are exalted into a position of authority, or covering, over what would be considered the "masses" or the lower class of people. Talk about taking away the importance of each member of the Body of Christ and establishing arrogant elitism in the leadership that is aggressive and unloving!

Clearly, this is the world's way of distinguishing the value and worth of people in regard to its organization and plans, but it is not God's way. We even have this warning from Peter to the elders concerning the local flocks of God, *"Feed the flock of God which is among you, taking the oversight of it, not by constraint but willingly; not for filthy lucre but of a ready mind; Neither as being*

---

[9] Nicolaitanism (The Rise and Growth of the Clergy), F. W. Grant, Believers Bookshelf Inc., pgs. 5, 9

lords over God's heritage, but being ensamples to the flock" (1 Peter 5:2-3).

The important question is what religious basis would Nicolaitanism use to bring the sheep of God into such bondage? Grant believes the answer lies in the environment that was prevalent. To understand environment, we must discern the spirit behind the Nicolaitans. Minister Frank Mceleny describes the spirit as thriving where there is no fear of God. It preaches freedom but enslaves, promotes unity but at the cost of truth. It claims to speak for Christ, yet it is the very doctrine He hates.

Scripture states that the Body at Pergamum was dwelling where Satan's seat or throne was located. He pointed out that Satan is not in hell; rather, he is reigning from his throne upon the earth. This point is firmly confirmed by such Scriptures as *Job 1:6-8*. Since Satan is the god of this world, the concept of dwelling where Satan's throne is implies settling down in the world.[10]

Clearly, the temptation for the Church to join the world was intense. With each passing year and generation, the resolve to maintain such a distinction from the world would become less and less. However, the new Church would not blatantly come into agreement with the world. There had to be some type of religious entanglement to bring the members into union or agreement. According to Grant, Satan's clever entanglement involved judaizing the Church.[11]

When you read the New Testament, such an attempt was not new. The Apostle Paul constantly confronted the inroads that Judaism subtly made into the new Church. After all, the logic was easy enough to present to any immature, zealous, or gullible Christian since the Law was of God. It was also God who ordained the rituals established by the Law; therefore, it was logical that it was something the new Church had to become subservient to in

---

[10] Ibid, pg. 3
[11] Ibid, pgs. 6-8

order to be identified as God's people. However, Paul was quite adamant that to become subservient to the Law in this fashion was to come back under the influence of the flesh. Christ's death on the cross did away with the ordinances (rituals) of the Law.

Jesus fulfilled every aspect of the Law. He now serves as the end of the Law for righteousness, thereby, serving as the righteousness of the believer. As believers, we are now justified by faith, which is accounted to us for righteousness. To walk according to the flesh would bring a person back under the law of sin and death. In the end, the very Law of God would condemn such an individual, not justify them.[12] This is why Paul made this statement in *Galatians 3:2b-3, "Received ye the Sprit by the works of the law, or by the hearing of faith? Are ye so foolish? Having begun in the Spirit, are ye now made perfect by the flesh?"*

To bring God's people under some type of clergy simply puts them under the traditions of those who have been exalted and given underserved authority to dictate to God's people how they are to believe, act, and express their devotion and worship before Him. Jesus encountered this with the scribes and the Pharisees. The scribes or lawyers of the Law were the ones who classified and arranged the Law's precepts. Clearly, these men would determine the intent or emphasis they wanted to bring out about something. Eventually, their words or conclusions became honored above the Law. The Pharisees were the ones who interpreted or explained the Law to the laity.[13]

The concept of the clergy/laity was clearly in operation during Jesus' day. The spirit or intent of the commandments of God was replaced with the traditions of the elders. These traditions were nothing more than the doctrines of men. They made converts to the religious system with its ridiculous petty rules and regulations,

---

[12] Matthew 5:17-18; Romans 3:28; 5:18; 8:2; 10:4; 1 Corinthians 1:30; Colossians 2:14

[13] Smiths Bible Dictionary; William Smith, Thomas Nelson Publishers

but not converts to the ways of the God of heaven. Jesus said of such traditions and doctrine that the place they held in people's lives actually put aside God's commandments.

It is important to point out that God's commandments remain in place, but many of the practices or rituals of the Law have been fulfilled in Christ. Traditions established by men become rituals that often change the intent or redefine how the commandments were to be honored. In other words, His commandments have been replaced, as men not only nullify their authority in the lives of God's people, but also reject them in preference to the traditions.[14]

When the world came into the Church, it succeeded in doing what the powers behind its religious systems had failed to do in the past. There was now a union between the Church and the world. The Church had now stepped out of its proper place into the environment of heathen idolatry, bringing it under the subtle influence of Satan. As a result, its leadership would now be redefined to make it subservient to the religious system's ways and agendas.

Since Constantine was emperor, as well as the one who spearheaded this new religious movement in his kingdom, it was obvious that he would become the new leader of this religion. In A. D. 325, he convened the first ecumenical council, called the Council of Nicea. He began to establish his agendas and practices at the expense of truth. Sadly, the Christians played into his design. They honored him as the Bishop of Bishops, while Constantine referred to himself Vicarius Christi or the Vicar of Christ.[15] In fact, Constantine became the Roman Catholic Church's first pope.

Constantine replaced Jesus in the new religion. He was the first ecumenist who tried to bring all the religions of his empire

---

[14] Mark 7:1-13
[15] A Woman Rides the Beast; © 1994 by Dave Hunt, pg. 46

under his auspice, regardless of the wrong spirit or perverted truth behind them. This system was a prelude to the antichrist, one-world system that will take center stage in the last days. Clearly, this setup was nothing more than Nicolaitanism, where the clergy was now exalted in position, power, and influence over the masses.

The digression created by this wicked system was even more realized in the Middle Ages. It was during this age of grave darkness upon the world that the bishops of Rome began to claim that they were the sole representatives of Christ upon the earth.[16] Ultimately, they replaced the position and work of the Holy Spirit in the visible Church in order to serve as the religious conscience of the people and the sole interpreters of God's Word.

This unholy union would eventually cause the professing Church to prove itself to be unfaithful to the Lord Jesus Christ. It would cause a mixture that would reshape the presentation of the Church in the minds of those who profess the name of Christ. Let us now consider how this has affected the "professing" Church.

Leadership: Nicolaitanism is alive and well in the professing Church. Granted, the names may have changed in relationship to the titles in which it may operate under, but it is alive. For example, it is now the modern-day apostles and prophets that are serving in the same positions that the scribes, Pharisees, and Sadducees held in Jesus' day. These false ministers even boldly declare that they are the covering over the Church, clearly deceiving those who come within their heretical grasp.

The positions of most elders and deacons have been reduced to operating as board members that simply work in a capacity of administration, but do not serve in a spiritual capacity. Sadly, those who hold many of these positions do so because of worldly prestige, and not because they fit the criteria set down in Scripture. Since the professing Church is out of order, the

---

[16] Ibid

heretical leadership of these various false ministers of righteousness has free reign to fleece the sheep, undermine the Word of God, and purport a different gospel. These false leaders also provide the platform for hireling shepherds and wolves to stand upon in the pulpits, gaining control of the hearts and minds of Jesus' fold.

Identification: The members of the true Church of Jesus Christ have three distinct identifying marks upon their lives. The first is the seal of the Holy Spirit. He identifies the members of the true Church with their eternal inheritance. The second identifying mark is separation. True Christianity entails separating from the world in order to separate unto God for His purpose and will.[17] The third identifying mark is true charity, benevolence, or love.

God's love entails both benevolence and charity. Jesus told His disciples that if they loved Him, they would obey His commandments. The three main commandments that were clearly stipulated by Jesus are fulfilled with one word—love.

Love is a commitment to God to be right before Him, an attitude of benevolence and compassion to do right by others, and acts of charity that reveal that the believers have truly become identified to the plight of those who are part of the household of faith. If this love is not present in a person's life, they cannot claim to be a true disciple of Jesus.[18]

Thanks to the attitude and influence of the world in the professing Church, the identifying marks have changed. Instead of clearly identifying true believers, the established marks of the visible Church are used to control and judge others. This judgment is now based on denominations, doctrines, and practices. For example, the typical concern of many professing Christians is not whether you are saved, but what denomination (church) you are affiliated with. This will classify or identify you as to whether you

---

[17] Ephesians 1:11-14; James 1:27
[18] Mark 12:29-31; John 13:34-35; 14:15; Romans 13:8-10; Galatians 6:2, 9-10

have any credibility and worth. It is important to point out there is no discernment in this type of judgment.

As you can see, the face of the Church has changed in the minds of many professing Christians. Even though the denomination did not die on the cross to save them, it is still regarded as the source of identification with salvation or truth. Membership to some denomination places you in the "in" church that is often presented as having the best corner on truth. Once again it matters little if a person's name is written in the Book of life, as long as they are associated with the acceptable denomination and are clearly jumping through the religious hoops.

The Bible does not make any reference to denominations, but local bodies of believers that find a common ground at the point of foundation (Jesus) and sweet fellowship in the Holy Spirit. As far as doctrine goes, we are to go on to perfection in our lives in Christ.

Doctrine will establish us in our lives in Christ, but it does not constitute our lives. To go on to perfection means to become enlightened to the ways of God, taste the heavenly gift of His life, and to be partakers of the Holy Spirit. To be partakers of the heavenly life in this way also points to tasting the good Word of God and the powers of the world or age to come.[19]

As we follow the idolatrous exaltation of denominations and man's doctrines, we can begin to see the digression of the visible Church, along with the worldly view it started to adopt. Denomination immediately associates a person with a particular doctrine. Doctrine will not only distinguish the beliefs that a person might hold to, but certain practices as well. With this in mind, it is clear that denomination has subtly become the way to salvation, doctrine has become the sacred cow that one dares not challenge or touch, and practices according to traditions have become marks that identify a person to a particular "elite" group, making a

---

[19] Hebrews 6:1-5

person or denomination superior to the masses. Jesus clearly rebuked such an attitude of sectarianism in His disciples.[20]

Each of these identifying marks of the worldly religious system not only exalts denomination over the leadership of Christ, doctrine over the Word of God, and traditions over the simple, practical ways of God's love, but it also creates the fruit of schisms in the professing Church.

Instead of believers being identified to their common ground of Jesus Christ, they become judgmental as they claim elitism over the masses that are not associated to their particular group. After all, they have the real answer to what is true, honorable, and acceptable to God. Although they classify others according to their denominations, interpret the Word of God through their doctrines, and take pride in their traditions, they have failed to see that such identification simply reveals that they are carnal or fleshly, and not counted as righteous.

The Corinthians had similar associations in their Body. They were classifying the validity of their Christianity and salvation based on those with whom they were associated. Some bragged that they were of Paul, while others took pride in being of Apollos. The Apostle Paul identified such schisms as being associated with envy and strife. Such works are carnal or of the flesh.[21]

It is important for Christians to realize that, if their identification goes back to any other person or source than the Lord Jesus Christ, they are still walking in the ways of the flesh and not according to the Spirit of God. The Holy Spirit has one responsibility. He is to lead believers into all truth about Jesus. It is from the premise of Jesus, that pure doctrine is established. Out of pure doctrine comes godly conduct that will make the believer

---

[20] Mark 9:38-41
[21] 1 Corinthians 3:1-4; Galatians 5:15-21

stand distinct from this world in disposition, attitude, and emphasis.[22]

When you consider what the best man can accomplish according to agreement with the world, it is easy to see how people become boxed in and conditioned by a religious system. Man now provides the spiritual covering. The denomination has become a ceiling that will determine how far a person will go in their pursuit of God and their understanding of godly service. Doctrine will serve as the idolatrous walls that will decide what a person will believe, as well as how they should interpret the Christian life. The practices of these religious boxes produce lifeless traditions that become the platforms that set a standard of self-righteousness. Such self-righteousness is nothing more than religious pride. As a result, many of God's sheep find themselves boxed in by an unseen entity that is lifeless, legalistic, indifferent, cruel, and unrealistic.

Experiences: The Christian life is meant to be experienced. However, it must be experienced in two arenas—the Spirit and according to God's truth. The natural man who operates in the flesh, according to the influence of the world, cannot discern the things of the Spirit.[23]

Since the Spirit is missing in most religious activities, there is spiritual leanness in many to discover the spiritual part of Christianity. The problem is that many of these individuals do not seek the truth out in Scripture.

We are told in *Romans 5:3-5* that experiences are part of the Christian life; but they are in light of the hope that awaits each of us in glory. Such experiences imply some type of trial that has taken place in our lives. Therefore, our understanding of God is disciplined by tribulation that works sobriety, patience that works character, and the assurance of hope that lives in expectation.

---

[22] John 16:12-15; Romans 6:17; 1 Timothy 4:6-8; Titus 2:10-12; 1 John 2:8-10
[23] 1 Corinthians 2:13-15

This will all be according to the godly love that must be present in our hearts.[24]

What most people are missing is a greater revelation of Jesus Christ that is alive and satisfying to the soul. It is in such revelation that they will experience the life, beauty, and glory of our Lord. Since these people have not learned that, in Christianity, a believer's main desire should be to know, see, and experience Christ in greater measure, they seek out spiritual experiences. The reason for their search is because of the wrong presentation of spiritual matters, and because such experiences are mistakenly associated with the presence and power of the Holy Spirit. However, the spiritual door these individuals walk through is not the door of truth, but the door of the occult.

Sadly, these occult experiences become more real than reality to these people. These experiences work a lot like a drug high. People find themselves always in need of another fix or mystic experience in the spiritual realm. In the end, everything will become subservient to these experiences, including the Word of God.

It is easy to see why the face of the professing Church has changed. It is in an identity crisis. When many people think of the Church of Jesus, they think in terms of a building or a denomination, but not according to the Word of God. They do not see that the Church is made up of people who are not associated with some particular denomination, doctrine, or practice, but who have become truly identified with the person and redemptive work of Jesus Christ.

What about you? Do you need to let your concept of Church go to the wayside in order to allow it to be revolutionized by the Word of God? Remember, Jesus did not die for a particular denomination, doctrine, or tradition. He died for people, for you and me. We must never allow any man, system, doctrine, or

---

[24] Strong Exhaustive Concordance of the Bible, #1382

tradition to replace or undermine our understanding of His salvation and our assurance because of it.

7

FOUNDATION REDEFINED

It is important to keep in mind that God has always had a people. In the Old Testament, it was a nation that was to represent His character and interests in that particular age. In today's age, the Lord has a Body or Church to proclaim His message, represent His kingdom, and do His bidding. Each of these entities were to clearly serve as the light in this dark world, bringing contrast and hope.

Every age has its own type of darkness. For the children of Israel, that darkness came in the form of blatant practices of idolatry and paganism. In Jesus' day, the present age was darkened by dead religion and internal power struggles between the different factions of the religious and worldly leaderships. In Paul's case, his particular mission field was darkened by various idols, temples, and philosophies that embraced everything the world offered, but were void of truth.

Each age or transition that the world has gone through had its own flavor of darkness that embraced its own brand of ignorance, unbelief, and deception. In each age, man's ignorance towards God was clouded by the different superstitions that had been thrust upon him by family, culture, and/or religious influences.[1] Each age of darkness added to the next age of delusion. Because of this darkness, man continues to walk in blatant unbelief towards

---

[1] The use of the word "man" is in relationship to both male and female.

God's Word, often deeming it obsolete or insignificant according to the present "enlightenment" that is in operation in the current age.

Ultimately, man will walk according to his own take on reality. This reality will be based on superstitions and the false light of the present age, but, nevertheless, it is the reality he will strive to bring about and maintain. However, it is all a lie that has blinded him to the real light of this world, Jesus Christ.

This brings us to the present age. How does the professing Church express itself now? Since the world is defining much of the visible Church, Christianity has become a subculture within the different cultures of the world.

It has its own language, as well as its own religious traditions and beliefs. It boxes people into its system to be conditioned according to the box's particular light, philosophies, agendas, and ways. Therefore, the professing Church is now part of the world's systems. Since it has become an integral part of the present age, the professing Church will ultimately fail to stand distinct in the present darkness.

Like any subculture, the worldly Christianity appears to have its beneficial points that will add to the mosaic of the world with its diverse cultures and practices. However, the organized Church will use the philosophies, measures, and methods of the world to try to attract people to its particular take on life.

For example, God's love no longer points to redemption, but to tolerance. Sin is no longer a terminal disease of the soul that has brought man under a death sentence, but it is simply a mistake, a physical illness, or an inherited trait that alleviates a person from any real Scriptural or moral accountability. Since God loves us, He wants us to be happy regardless of the fornication or unholy agreement we may commit in our lives to secure some exaggerated, so-called "happiness".

Needless to say, these are blatant lies, but they are affecting the attitudes of believers. The truth is that God's main desire is that we partake of His holiness so that we are able to see Him.[2] But, these compromising attitudes show us that there is a mixture in operation.

These mixtures are revealing how worldly the professing Church has become. Sadly, the best each individual can do in this environment is to tack Christ on to all of their activities as a way to deceive themselves about their true spiritual condition.

As I have considered the struggles of the professing Church, I have realized that it has always been the same throughout the different transitions that have taken place throughout the ages. The real Church that Jesus died for must come back to center, but, first, it must recognize how the darkness of the present age is affecting it. The struggle to come back to center does not occur without some type of travail taking place within the souls of believers.

As with all travail, it begins with restlessness. The soul is no longer comfortable with what is considered normal in the religious scene. Something is being stirred in the believer. The believer may not understand the stirring, but it has to do with the very life of Christ coming to its fullness in their life. His life must be birthed, established, consecrated, or revived in a person, depending upon their spiritual status. For example, Christ' life must come forth from the womb of the heart or from the grave of the lifeless soul where the work or regeneration and sanctification has been stifled in some way.

The stirring behind this life is the Holy Spirit. Once the restlessness begins, then the process for this new or renewed life must take place. Life that comes forth in the heart, or innermost being within a person, points to a lost soul being saved from the clutches of God's wrath through the new-birth (born-again)

---

[2] Hebrews 12:14

experience. However, for the tomb that represents the poor substitute of lifeless religion, where the breath of God has been grieved, quenched, or vexed, this new life coming forth points to reformation and/or revival.

For the renewed life to come forth in power and glory, it will take revolution, suffering, persecution, and/or death. As you study the history of God's people, much of the renewal of life came from the premise of reformation.

One of the greatest reformations in Israel occurred during the reign of King Hezekiah.[3] The temple doors had been closed to the life, truth, and ways of God. Hezekiah opened the doors of the temple and called the priests and Levites back into the work of service. Their first order of business was to cleanse themselves so that they could cleanse and sanctify the temple. Hezekiah also called the remainder of the people of Israel back to their former roots by observing the Passover.

Reformation usually begins when there has been personal revival within the one who is spearheading it. Hezekiah had a personal renewal take place in his life. Renewal or revival involves a renewing of vision and purpose. Only the Holy Spirit can revive or renew a vision, while man can only reform what is wrong in order to encourage an environment of revival for others.

Revival involves an awakening to one's spiritual condition. This awakening leads to brokenness that produces humility, repentance, conversion, and consecration. Reformation is the means to reform the beliefs, ways, or practices of a body or group of people that have left their original function or purpose. In Hezekiah's situation, he was trying to reform a nation that belonged to Jehovah God. This involved ridding the land of all idolatrous and abominable practices.

Reformation in the religious arena begins at the point of personal faith. Genuine faith will lead the person back to God and

---

[3] 2 Kings 18-19; 2 Chronicles 29-31

His Word. They will choose to believe the Word, and will come back to the center in regard to God's truth. It is at the point of this faith that God can revive a person with a greater revelation of Jesus and His redemption. It is important to point out that revival occurs when people truly begin to have a personal revelation of how much their sin truly cost God. At this point, people are broken in their arrogance and self-sufficiency, and, in repentance and desperation, they begin to seek God's mercy.

As we study reformation and revival, people can reform without being spiritually revived. In other words, they can change their minds and practices without spiritual renewal. This is why it is important to understand the difference between these two environments. Reformation can result in personal revival for those who are seeking change in their lives or have tender hearts towards God, but such revival will not necessarily sweep the masses.

However, revivals that are clearly being spearheaded by the Holy Spirit are like great waves that sweep the masses into their powerful grip. The most unlikely people can end up falling on their knees in total repentance, seeking forgiveness, being converted to the righteous ways of God, and total consecrating from their wicked ways in order to be sanctified unto God by His Spirit.

Reformation calls for change, while revival produces brokenness and consecration. Reformation can cause people to see the need to change the face of what is going on in the religious environment, but revival often allows people to feel and smell the very fires of hell nipping at their heals, causing a transformation of the inward environment that is conducive for real revival and total abandonment to God.

This brings us back to the activities of the Church. Throughout the years there have been various reformers such as Martin Luther. These reformers came forth as firebrands in the midst of lifeless religion. The stirring that occurred in these men began at the point of faith in God's Word. They chose to believe simple truths such as "the just shall live by faith" and "that salvation is matter of God's grace and not man's works."[4]

These reformers recognized that they could not reform the Catholic Church; therefore, they had to step outside of the system to bring truth and liberty to the poor burdened souls. Repercussions followed.

The Catholic Church set out to persecute and silence these firebrands. However, this religious system could not silence the Word of God. It continued to be the source of liberty for those who sought truth among its pages, even within the midst of grave ignorance, lifeless traditions, and possible persecution.

In our Church history, we also have those who were used to bring forth great tidal waves of revival. There are two fires that can burn through the Church—persecution and the Holy Spirit. The fires of persecution often refine faith among the members of Jesus' Body, bringing much needed cleansing and purging. However, the Spirit is what sets the soul aflame with resolve and passion. The resolve is to ensure that one is right before God, while there is passion to fulfill the calling, vision, or commission out of loving devotion. Those who are associated with the great moves of the Spirit upon the saved and the unsaved alike are men with such names as Whitefield, Edwards, Roberts, and Finney.

Whether in times of reformation or revival, these men had one thing in common—they had stepped outside of the box established by the carnal religious influences of man and the sensual practices of the world to personally encounter God.

At such times the true Church of Jesus had the opportunity to get its bearings. However, there was always controversy that followed the reformers and revivalists. They both posed a threat to the rule, control, and influence of the religious system upon the hearts and minds of the people.

---

[4] Romans 1:17; Ephesians 2:8-10

In times of such controversy, where the fires of persecution and oppression are fanned in an attempt to try to buffet the reformation of the firebrands or the powerful moving of the Spirit, the true Church of Jesus is often clearly refined and established. In such movements of reformation or revival, the choices are made clear. There are no gray areas of worldly compromise or uncertainty. People not only clearly see the difference between man's religion and the Lord's Body, but they realize that there is a cost to be part of the Living Church of Jesus Christ.

Once again, we must come back to how the world influenced the Church. We know that when the Holy Spirit is missing, then an environment will be in place for the shifting of leadership. After all, man now can step into place as the spiritual conscience of others and condition them to embrace the religious box designed by fallen man. In this light, man can now subtly replace the Head as the one who holds the authority over the Church as sovereign leader. In such a place, the right leader will take hold of the minds of the people.

Now that man has taken hold of the minds to influence people's point of view to conform to his way of thinking and attitudes towards God, he can now control their practices and behaviors. In this position, he can replace service to God with service to the cause of the religious system or to worldly inspired leadership. It is at this point that the foundation can be redefined.

According to the Apostle Paul, there is only one foundation upon which we can successfully build our spiritual lives. This foundation is known as the Rock. This Rock serves as the stone that will break us at the point of our independent dispositions, or it will crush us into powder with judgment. Not only is a believer's life firmly established upon this immovable Rock of ages, but also the Spirit of God is building the true Church upon it, as the Lord personally adds living stones to this living organism.[5] We are

---

[5] Matthew 7:24-27; 16:18; 21:42-44; Acts 2:47; 1 Corinthians 3:11; 10:4

reminded once again that man has no real part in actually building the Church of Jesus. He may be a vessel that is used to preach the message of salvation, but he does not actually build the house.

As you consider that there is **one foundation** upon which the Body is established, there should and will be agreement rather than schisms. There is only **one true Spirit** of God who works in accordance to the plans of heaven; therefore, there should never be debates about what is right and acceptable. Since there is **only one hope** that is being established within the heart of the Body, there should not be any confusion about what we need to pursue as true followers of Christ.

As the Body is firmly anchored in place by one hope, its calling will be brought forth according to its **one Lord or Owner**. This **one calling** will be developed and refined by the **one faith** that was first delivered to the saints who were baptized into the Body by the Holy Spirit. Such baptism is done according to the plan of the Father, who is above all, through all, and in all through the presence of His Spirit in those who belong to the true Body of the Lord Jesus Christ.[6]

The Apostle Paul clearly identifies that the one true foundation is the Lord Jesus Christ. In the previous chapter of this book, it was presented how false apostles and prophets are presenting themselves as ministers of righteousness. It was also brought out that there are hireling shepherds and wolves standing behind many pulpits. Such facts will not escape those who are guarding the truth. But it must be noted that such heretics are not only motivated by the wrong spirit of the world, but they are open doors or avenues by which this wrong spirit will seduce others into an unholy agreement to embrace doctrines of devils.[7]

It is important to understand that, in such an environment, the foundation can be redefined without people recognizing the error.

---

[6] Ephesians 4:3-6
[7] 1 Corinthians 3:11; 1 Timothy 4:1-2

As I have already established, the foundation is not a matter of denomination, beliefs, or rituals, but the Person of the Lord Jesus Christ.

When it comes to the one true foundation of every Christian, they must realize that true agreement can only be obtained at the point of what has been established as the true common ground for all believers—Jesus. However, the Lord Jesus Christ is not just any "old" Jesus. In other words, He is not a figment of someone's imagination or a faceless person who lived, and who those of the religious arena can define in any old way that serves their religious causes or emphasis.

The Jesus I am talking about was clearly unveiled in Scripture through shadows, prophecies, and teachings. This very same Jesus stated that He was the only way to heaven. He also warned that, in the end days, many different "messiahs" would be presented, but, as His followers, we are not to give them any audience or follow them into their different delusions.[8]

Jesus brought out this very important issue with His disciples when He asked them a simple question in *Matthew 16:13b, "Who do men say that I, the Son of man, am?"* I have dealt with this subject many times. However, we must understand why the visible Church is in its present spiritual condition.

Others always influence our initial understanding of God, Jesus, and life. The tendency, in our limited box of understanding, is to assume that whatever we have been told must be correct. After all, our family, church, or religious leaders have conditioned us in our thinking, and they would not lie to us.

Take it from a former cult member; each of these sources could very well lie to you. The reason for such a lie is because many of these sources have also been blinded to the truth of Jesus Christ by their influences that keep them in their own ignorance and unbelief. They are operating from an assumption

---

[8] Matthew 24:4-5, 23-27; John 14:6; Acts 4:12; Colossians 2:14-17

and not from the premise of truth. To confirm this point, the disciples' answer proved that people speculate much about Jesus, but they fail to discover who He is for themselves. *"And they said, Some say that thou art John the Baptist; some, Elijah, and others, Jeremiah, or one of the prophets" (Matthew 16:14).*

Let us consider for a moment the environment in which Jesus lived in His humanity. The Jewish people were looking for their Messiah, but many held to the concept that Jesus was John the Baptist or some other prophet that rose from the dead.[9] These people were looking for the Messiah, but, when He stood in front of them, they still did not recognize Him. As a result, they were wrong about who He was.

My family and religion were both wrong about Jesus. Since I believed them, I was wrong as well. My whole foundation was wrong. Therefore, my whole premise on which I regarded God, considered Jesus, and viewed life was wrong! The problem with being wrong in this situation is that it would have cost me my very soul if I had failed to get it right.

In my former perspective, God was a vague concept because the cult I attended had subtly replaced Him. I had a sentimental notion of Jesus as a baby in a manger, otherwise there was confusion. The reason for this confusion was that the only time I took note of Him in a religious way was in regard to how the men of my religion were purported to actually serve as a "Christ" in their families. In fact, they were the ones who would supposedly call their wives from the grave. Therefore, I was encouraged to prepare to marry so I could have my own personal "Christ" that would be sure to not leave me in that terrible place of the grave.

To those who maintain beliefs about Jesus, such a delusional belief on the part of my former cult would seem absolutely ridiculous, but, in all honesty, how do each of us know if our understanding about Jesus is correct? How many of us assume

---

[9] Matthew 16:14

we know Him, but, in reality, we do not have a clue? Jesus is not an intellectual, religious concept that has been rendered lifeless and without dimension by the knowledge and philosophies of religion and the world; rather, He is a revelation of the heart to those who truly believe. He is alive and reigns as Lord and King within the hearts of those who love Him.

Jesus then asked the disciples the next question in *Matthew 16:15b, "But who say ye that I am?"* Jesus was now making it a personal matter. He in fact, was speaking to each of us. *"Who do you say that I am?"* Peter answered Him correctly, but it is important to note how Peter received such an understanding. It was not based upon his intellectual or religious understanding. Jesus told Peter that the Father in heaven revealed to Peter His real identity.[10]

The Bible is clear. We must believe the record it has given to us about the true Jesus.[11] Such a record is made revelation to the receptive heart. It is from the correct premise of who Jesus is that the Christian life is clearly founded and established.

Who is the real Jesus? Peter gave us some insight in his answer in *Matthew 16:16b, "Thou art the Christ, the Son of the living God."* Peter was acknowledging that Jesus was the Promised One who would come to deliver the Jewish people. However, this deliverance was not to be a physical deliverance from the oppression of the Gentile rulers, but a spiritual deliverance from oppression caused by sin.

As the Promised One, He was also the King of the Jews. Instead of reestablishing Israel as a physical kingdom, He came to establish a spiritual kingdom that would live within the hearts of men. As the Messiah, He was anointed to carry out a work that would result in the spiritual healing, reconciliation, and restoration of man back into a relationship with God.

---

[10] Matthew 16:17
[11] 1 John 5:9-13

81

Unlike what I was told by my former cult, Jesus is the only Christ, and, as *John 5:21-29* clearly stipulates, He is the One who will call people out of the grave, either unto everlasting life or eternal damnation. This brings us to the second aspect of Jesus. He is the Son of the Living God.

As the Messiah, we get insight into His work and mission as man. But, as the Son of the Living God, we get insight into His nature and character. We know that, as the Messiah, He came as man to fulfill His mission as the Lamb of God. However, He is also divine by nature. He has the same nature and status as the Father, making Him equal to Him. However, when He was fashioned as a man in the womb of a woman, He gave up His sovereignty as God, thereby, ceasing to be equal with God[12]

The Apostle John clearly brings Jesus' deity out in the first three verses of the first chapter of his Gospel when he identifies the Living Word as being God. He summarizes this revelation in *John 1:14, "And the Word was made flesh, and dwelt among us (and we beheld his glory, the glory as of the only begotten of the Father), full of grace and truth."*

The Apostle Paul also summarized Jesus' identity as well as His entrance as man into the world. In *1 Timothy 1:17*, Paul described the Lord in this way, *"Now unto the King eternal, immortal, invisible, the only wise God, be honor and glory forever and ever. Amen."* As King, Jesus has always existed (eternal). He is immortal, exempt from ceasing to exist. He is invisible, because He operates in the unseen world, yet He lives. He is the only wise God who deserves to be honored and glorified forever.

The Apostle Paul summarized Jesus' entrance into this world in *1 Timothy 3:16, "And without controversy great is the mystery of godliness: God was manifest in the flesh, justified in the Spirit, seen of angels, preached unto the Gentiles, believed on in the world, received up into glory."* God becoming man was a great

---

[12] John 5:17-18; Philippians 2:5-8

mystery of godliness. He was manifested in the flesh, confirmed by the Spirit, witnessed by the host of heaven, preached among those who were considered rejected, believed on by those who were in the world, and received up into glory. Such a mystery can only be unveiled to those who are pure in heart and are prepared to believe, by faith, the record that the Word of God has clearly set forth about the Son of God.

It is this incredible revelation of Jesus that makes up the true foundation. If we do not believe every aspect of this Scriptural record, we will end up possessing a different Jesus. Such a Jesus will be unable to save us. After all, the Father only recognizes His only begotten Son, not a Jesus who is a figment of someone's imagination. The Father even confirmed Jesus' identity on two different occasions—at His baptism and transfiguration. Both times, he introduced Jesus as His Son, fulfilling a prophecy found in *Psalm 2:7*.[13] The writer of Hebrews brought this into an interesting focus when he pointed out that the Father even referred to Jesus as God in *Hebrews 1:8, "But unto the Son he saith, Thy throne, O God, is forever and ever; a scepter of righteousness is the scepter of thy kingdom."*[14]

Today there are many different "messiahs" being presented. Some presentations are blatant heresy, while others possess some truth. But ninety-nine percent of them strip Jesus of His deity. He may be a great man, but He is not God in the flesh. He may be a great prophet, but He is not God Incarnate. He may be spiritual, but He is only a created being like the angels, rather than the Creator. He is the brother of Lucifer who simply presented a better plan, rather than the only one who could fulfill the plan of redemption. He died on the cross, but He is not compassionate

---

[13] Matthew 3:17; 17:5

[14] If you like to in-depth study about the identity of Jesus, see the author's book titled, *Unmasking the Cult Mentality.* It also contains a bonus book, *He Thought it Not Robbery* that also unveils the revelation of Christ in Philippians 2:5-11.

enough to be the sole mediator between God and man; therefore, He needs His biological mother to share such a position with Him.[15] In some cases, Jesus never gets past the manger in Bethlehem to die on the cross. In other cases, He never gets off the cross to prove victory over death in His resurrection. He is forever a baby that can bring sentimental tears to our eyes once a year, or He is always paying the price for our sins because His work on the cross was not enough to secure redemption.

Obviously, the reality behind the organized religions of the world is that they cannot let Jesus be Jesus. They oppose Him in subtle ways so they can define Him according to their purpose and agendas. Most of the religions of the world will not outright reject Christ; rather, they will use Him to attract people to a substitute Jesus that has no power to save their souls. Ultimately, these false religions define the spiritual foundation to fit their particular religious boxes.

The struggle in Christianity is to make sure our lives, as believers, are founded upon the correct Jesus. It has been an incredible journey for me to wade through the many religious presentations of Jesus. There are those confusing the real Christ by presenting a picture-perfect presentation of the Jesus of the Bible, but when you strip away the initial image, the real Jesus has been rendered useless by the legalistic propaganda and pagan practices of the religious systems that are hiding behind His name or concept.

Another popular Jesus is the worldly Jesus who is here to make people feel good about themselves, as well as do their bidding. There is the New Age Jesus who is simply one of the way-showers, since all the religious paths supposedly lead to God. There is also the Jesus who is the mystic. This counterfeit has no practical side to His life and ministry, especially since Christianity is nothing more than a mystical experience.

---

[15] 1 Timothy 2:5-6

We could go on and on about the different presentations of Jesus that are being offered, but there is only one Jesus that is truly the Son of God. He came by way of a simple virgin, a handmaiden that recognized her own need for a savior. He entered into the world via a manger. He was hidden in obscurity for the first thirty years of His life, became identified to man in the waters of baptism, and was tempted in the wilderness by Satan. In His, ministry He turned the world upside down, was crucified by religion, lifted up on the cross by a political system of the world, and treated like a common criminal by those who were ignorant of Him or feared and hated Him.

This Jesus was both the Christ and the Son of God. Since God promised a deliverer, Jesus stepped out of eternity and took on the likeness of man in order to redeem mankind from the harsh taskmasters of sin and death. As the Lamb of God, He was offered upon the altar of the cross where He paid the price for our sins. As God, He rose three days later from the grave to prove victorious over the sting of sin.

Jesus is fully man and fully God. Today, in His capacity as Man, He serves as our example, High Priest, and Mediator. However, as God, He reminds us of His unchangeable character and His power to save us. As Man, we see the compassion of God in His ways, but, as God, we are reminded that we can only meet God at the points of covenant, forgiveness, atonement, and reconciliation. As Man, He fits the criteria of being the only place in which reconciliation can take place with the Father, but, as God, we are reminded that, one day, He will come back as Judge of all, and He will judge according to His righteousness.

The other aspect of our foundation is that we will be discovering the extent of God's grace for ages to come.[16] We can never possess the complete revelation of Jesus, but we can be

---

[16] Ephesians 2:7

full of His life, always being enlarged to receive greater measures of Him.

Is your life founded upon the right Jesus, or will your foundation crumble in the fires of judgment? Is your foundation lifeless due to a mixture of spirit, man's influence, and the world, or is it living because the Holy Spirit is bringing revelation of our Lord's character, life, and ways to your spirit? Only you can answer these questions, but remember that, without the right foundation, you will not stand in the day of adversity and judgment, nor will God recognize you as belonging to the true Church of Jesus Christ.

8

CORNERSTONE READJUSTED

When man begins to replace the leadership of the Head, as well as the tender conscience of the Spirit, and begins to define the source or purpose behind life in the Body of Christ, he has free rein to redefine the foundation. We know Jesus is the only true foundation to every believer. Therefore, man will redefine Jesus to fit his particular emphasis, doctrine, or religious cause. As Jesus is redefined, He will lose the preeminence He must hold in the minds of His people.[1] Sadly, another Jesus will be presented in His place. However, this Jesus is a counterfeit that will not be recognized by God, the Father, as well as those who make up the true Church of Jesus Christ.

To redefine Jesus means to strip the foundation of eternal life of its stability or authority to stand as a shining beacon. Without the stability, the foundation will eventually collapse. Since every foundation will be shaken, each faulty foundation stands already doomed, and, when the winds of judgment finally come, that which is not firmly established upon the Rock will fall into total ruin.[2]

It is at the points of attempting to replace the foundation or the shaking of it that the visible Church will prove to be vulnerable. After all, the cement (Spirit) that holds the foundation together will

---

[1] Colossians 1:15-19
[2] Matthew 7:24-27; Hebrews 12:27-29

be missing, and the truths of Jesus that make up this foundation will be undermined by an unholy mixture. However, the true foundation must be stripped of its stability (authority) before the cornerstone of the Church can be readjusted to fit the purpose and cause of those who are trying to gain power over God's people.

The Bible is clear that Jesus also serves as our cornerstone.[3] It is important to understand how the character, life, ministry, and function of the believer and the Church are all found in Christ. As our Head, He ensures that our lives will function according to the will of God. As our foundation, He establishes us according to the authority of His nature and work of redemption. However, as our cornerstone, He determines how our life will line up to His life, attitude, examples, and teachings.

In my study of cornerstones, I realize that structures are designed according to the cornerstone. Based on the information about the temple of Solomon, all the stones were constructed outside of the temple and brought to the building site. These stones were all shaped according to the cornerstone.

There is a legend that even Jesus made reference to regarding the cornerstone of the temple of Solomon. It says that the builders did not recognize the cornerstone.[4] It was an odd shape compared to the rest of the stones. Therefore, the builders considered the stone to be a mistake and cast it down into their garbage dump. When they placed all of the stones into their rightful place, they discovered that the odd shaped stone they had discarded was the actual cornerstone. They had to dig it out of the dump in order to complete the temple.

This is how the Church of Jesus is built. It is designed according to His pattern that He clearly laid out in His life and ministry. Sadly, like many of the present builders of the Church, the Jews of Jesus' day refused to recognize Him as the only true

---

[3] 1 Peter 2:5-8
[4] Matthew 21:42

spiritual cornerstone, rejected Him and then cast Him into the grave. However, Jesus is the cornerstone of all truth, as well as the cornerstone to which all of the living stones of the Church are designed to line up to. He was not only raised from the grave to prove victorious over death, but He also took His rightful place as the cornerstone of His Church.[5]

As our foundation, Jesus enables us to stand against the storms brought against us by the kingdom of darkness. We are empowered to stand against the attacks aimed at God's truth by standing on the truth of who Jesus is. This is where our authority comes from against the powers of darkness. We will never be moved from who Jesus is, for He will never change.[6]

As our cornerstone, Jesus enables us to withstand the onslaught of heretical and demonic teachings and movements that come against His very life that is being formed within us by the sanctifying work of the Holy Spirit. The foundation of Jesus will affect how we view God, which will influence our attitudes and approach regarding Him. However, as our cornerstone, our lifestyle will be affected. In fact, the life in us must line up to the cornerstone to ensure consistency between our claims, our walk, and our fruits. The cornerstone we line up to will, in turn, affect how we view our lives, responsibilities, and places in the kingdom of God.

The problem for many Christians is that there is no connection between their claims of what they believe (foundation) and the life they live (structure). The lack of such a connection will classify such believers as hypocrites. The reason for the inconsistency is unbelief. It takes faith to connect the foundation of who Jesus is to the structure or life that is being established by the Spirit of God. Since His Word is a matter of truth it must be applied by faith to

---

[5] Romans 10:9-10; 1 Peter 2:5-8
[6] Hebrews 13:8

every aspect of our lives.[7] Application of the truth in this manner is what lines believers up to Jesus as the cornerstone, while ensuring that the living stones are being firmly established upon who He is.

When the connection of faith is missing between the foundation and the structure, you end up with a lopsided structure that is already doomed to collapse. The structure is worthless since it is not being established upon the proper foundation. It is easy to witness this inconsistency.

There are those who display religious piousness in the religious realm, but they are not firmly established upon the foundation. Eventually, different aspects of their lives will begin to collapse because there is no real foundation to what they believe or are advocating. Even though some of the structure is intact, it will still prove to be worthless when it comes to withstanding any of the storms that may be blowing through the religious world.

This brings us to the construction of the structure. The true builder of this structure is not man, but God. Granted, man is a co-laborer with God as far as establishing or reinforcing this spiritual structure upon the true foundation of Jesus, but the building must be according to the design of the Father and under the auspice of the ever-abiding, watchful care of the Spirit.[8] *Psalm 127:1* tells us that, unless the Lord builds the house, man's labor will be in vain. *Philippians 1:6* clearly established that it is God's good or beneficial work that is taking place in us. As a result, the Apostle Paul gave this warning, *"But let every man take heed how he buildeth upon it" (1 Corinthians 3:10c).*

What is being established in the inward sanctuary of man and within Jesus' Church should be His life. The Apostle Paul confirmed this when he stated, *"I am crucified with Christ: nevertheless I live; yet not I, but Christ liveth in me; and the life*

---

[7] Romans 10:17; Hebrews 11:6
[8] 1 Corinthians 3:9; Hebrews 3:4

which I now live in the flesh I live by the faith of the Son of God, who loved me and gave himself for me" (Galatians 2:20).

For the very life of Christ to be established in me, I must line up to the cornerstone. This means I will allow the very attitude of Christ to be developed in my life.[9] The attitude of Christ is one of meekness. Godly meekness will always come into submission to the will and plan of God.

To line up to the cornerstone means I will actually take on the very disposition of Christ. He was lowly or humble.[10] This made Him a servant before the Father, always ready to serve man for the glory of the Father.

Part of lining up to the cornerstone is following the pattern or example that Jesus left His followers. The Apostle John made this statement in *1 John 2:6, "He that saith he abideth in him ought himself also so to walk, even as he walked."*

Jesus left two major patterns for us to follow. However, we cannot follow these patterns unless we abide in the Vine. Such abiding is how the very life of Christ is imparted to us. As His life comes forth, we will develop His mind and take on His disposition. His mind will inspire us, and His disposition will discipline us.

Although I have mentioned these two examples many times before in my teachings and books, we must consider them in light of lining up to the cornerstone. The first example is found in *John 13:13-17.* The example is that of servitude. Jesus took on the disposition of a servant. In so doing, He permitted Himself to be abased as He allowed Himself to be fashioned as a man.

All of us are servants to something or someone, but the critical issue is who we are serving. If we give in to our natural preferences, we will be serving the spirit or god of this world. However, if we take our life back from the dictates of sin and consecrate it to God, we will serve God. The first type of service,

---

[9] Philippians 2:5
[10] Matthew 11:29

service to Satan, is a matter of just giving way to what is natural, fleshly, convenient, and comfortable. The second type of service involves submission that will bring a person into subjection to God. Godly submission is a powerful form of inward discipline.

True servants are disciplined by their very service. However, Jesus' example calls for inward discipline that truly commits all to God for His glory. As Jesus stated, *"The servant is not greater than his lord; neither he that is sent greater than he that sent him. If ye know these things, happy are ye if ye do them" (John 13:16b-17).*

Jesus showed us the secret of happiness as His servants. True submission simply comes into deference to that which is worthy for the benefit of the whole.[11] Such submission will ultimately put everyone in the Body on equal footing as they come into line with the cornerstone. After all, each spiritual building brick in our lives, and in the Church, is as important as the cornerstone to complete the whole of the building. If we understand this, we will discover true happiness. After all, we will have the freedom to step over our insipid pride, deny ourselves of personal rights to have life on our terms, and truly follow Jesus into a glorious life.

Godly submission also brings us under the yoke of Christ. The yoke will work the very disposition of Christ in us as it disciplines our walk. His yoke will prove to be easy because it is about doing the will of the Father out of love and for His glory. It will also bring about spiritual maturity as we continue to understand what it means to grow up in Christ, who is our Head.[12]

The second pattern that Jesus left us can be found in *1 Peter 2:21-22, "For even hereunto were ye called, because Christ also suffered for us, leaving us an example, that ye should follow his steps; Who did no sin, neither was guile found in his mouth."* We can clearly see Jesus' mind or attitude in these Scriptures. He was

---

[11] Ephesians 5:21
[12] Matthew 11:29-30; Ephesians 4:15

willing to give way to suffering in order to fulfill the will of the Father. He refused to sin, or to open His mouth in defense of His innocence, or rebuke His false accusers. In meekness, He came into obedience as the Lamb of God to be led to the slaughter. This suffering was vital to bring Him forth in perfection in His humanity as a means to bring about the way of salvation.[13]

Hebrews 5:8-9 gives us this insight, *"Though he were a Son, yet learned he obedience by the things which he suffered; And being made perfect, he became the author of eternal salvation unto all them that obey him."* Godly meekness allows us to learn obedience. However, true obedience comes with a cost. The first cost is that one must deny self to truly obey. The second cost is coming under the spiritual burden ordained by God to see His plan fulfilled.

Jesus came under the burden of the cross. The burden we are asked to carry is light. It is the burden of love. Love is the only way to fulfill the plan of God. It is what inspires or compels us to walk out the Christian life. It is selfless and sacrificial. It always expresses itself in meekness.[14] In other words, its strengths, passions, and devotion are disciplined by godly meekness. This meekness is the product of being under the control of the Spirit.

Since the world came into the Church, it is hard for believers to understand that, unless their mind is transformed, their attitude and disposition will not be fully regenerated. The Apostle Paul stated that the mind is conformed to this world's way of thinking; therefore, it must be transformed by the renewing of the Spirit.[15]

Due to the influence of the world upon the professing Church's way of thinking, some Christians fail to see the problem that is clearly besetting the Church. Since there are no absolutes about

---

[13] Isaiah 53:7

[14] Matthew 11:29-30; Romans 5:5; 13:8-10; 1 Corinthians 13; 2 Corinthians 5:14-15; Ephesians 4:12-16

[15] Romans 12:2

the identity of Jesus as the true spiritual foundation, He can now be adjusted to fit people's particular lifestyles. Therefore, any concept of Him will be brought into submission to cultural preferences, lined up to religious pursuits, and presented according to worldly taste. In essence, He is being tacked on to man's activities, attuned to religious agendas, dressed according to personal preferences, and designed according to worldly, popular images. For example, to the businessman, He is the most successful CEO. To the punk rocker, He is tattooed and dressed according to the taste of those presenting Him. To the surfer, He is presented as the coolest surfer of the present age. To the politician, He is anyone you want to make Him to be since we live in a tolerant society. In summation, He has been blended into every culture and race, stripping Him of all distinction.

Clearly, if the foundation has been redefined, then Jesus, as the cornerstone, can be adjusted to fit the present age. Shamefully, the different presentations of Jesus make Him part of the world and its activities. Even though Jesus stated that He came from above and was not of this world, He is now presented from a worldly premise. Of course, such unholy adjustments are justified in the name of Christ and for the sake of furthering the Gospel.

When we consider Jesus as our cornerstone, we must realize that our lives are meant to be shaped according to the cornerstone; rather than the cornerstone being adjusted to fit our particular lifestyles. It is important to understand that most people are being allowed to define the Christian life according to a worldly presentation of Christianity. The main reason for this is because there is no true discipleship taking place in many of the Christian churches.

If the foundation is wrong, then there is no means by which to properly disciple a person. True discipleship is what properly lines the person up to Jesus as the cornerstone. However, much of the discipleship involves establishing or reinforcing the foundation of who Jesus is and must be in our lives. Subsequently, Christians' lifestyles will adjust according to their attitudes about life. If they do not have a proper perspective about the Lord, then they will fail to have the right attitude to properly line their lives up to His life, teachings, and examples. For this reason, the Apostle Paul, in essence, told us to work out our salvation in the attitude of fear and trembling.[16]

The other important part about the cornerstone is that it will also determine our reality. Jesus is the essence of truth. If a matter does not line up to Him, then it must be discarded. In order to line up to the truth, as Christians, we must operate in reality to properly test and discern both the spirit and fruits of our personal lives. This reality check is also necessary when it comes to testing the spirit and fruits of our different religious experiences and encounters.

When people adjust the cornerstone to fit their own reality, they are lining up to their own form of darkness or delusion, rather than truth. Jesus best described this state of affairs in *John 3:19-20*, *"And this is the condemnation, that light is come into the world, and men loved darkness rather than light, because their deeds were evil. For everyone that doeth evil hateth the light, neither cometh to the light, lest his deeds should be reproved."*

When you consider the lives of those who have erected their own cornerstone, you are able to see that nothing really fits. Not only are their lives not properly in line with truth, but they also are not firmly established upon the foundation. Not only are certain aspects of their lives ready to collapse from the lack of a foundation, but their actual structure also has no real design or order to it.

The pillars of their belief systems are crooked from inconsistencies, the walls that fortify their spiritual claims are warped due to hypocrisy, and the floors that make up their source

---

[16] Philippians 2:12

of reliance slant from the mixture of self-sufficiency and man-made religion.

As Christians, our lives are not meant to be attractive to the world, but to stand distinct from it. In order to stand distinct from the world, Christians must understand that their lives are to serve as the standard in which the Lord Jesus Christ is lifted up in distinction above the world. It is from this vantage point that people will be drawn to His character, work, and life.[17]

The only way a Christian can ensure that Jesus is lifted up in this manner is to take on His life so that they can reflect His glory from their disposition. The Apostle Paul talked about reflecting Jesus' glory. However, he also recognized that he had to cease living his personal life in order to live the life of Christ by faith.[18] I have often told other believers that I do not care to see them; rather, I desire to see Jesus being reflected from their lives.

What kind of life is being established within you? As a believer, it must be the life of Christ. However, His life cannot be established within you unless you are firmly planted upon Him as the foundation and are actively lining your life up to Him as the cornerstone.

---

[17] John 12:32
[18] 2 Corinthians 3:18; Galatians 2:20

96

9

PERVERTING
THE GOSPEL

It is important to follow the breakdown that is occurring in the religious realm. It is obvious why some of the Church of Jesus Christ would suffer an identity crisis. Such breakdowns of this nature occur slowly through small ways. For the professing Church, it started by simply changing the perspective about the Church or Body of Jesus. Instead of being composed of people, now it is often identified by denominational affiliation or some type of religious system or movement.

Once the perspective is changed about the makeup of the Church, then leadership in the Body can be redefined. Man and religion can now subtly replace Jesus as the Head and foundation of His Church, allowing people to adjust the cornerstone of all true religion to their own personal religious realities. The Apostle Paul penned his concerns about this matter in *2 Corinthians 11:3-4,*

> *But I fear, lest by any means, as the serpent beguiled Eve through his subtilty, so your minds should be corrupted from the simplicity that is in Christ. For if he that cometh preacheth another Jesus, whom we have not preached, or if ye receive another spirit, which ye have not received, or another gospel, which ye have not accepted, ye might well bear with him.*

"Bear" in this Scripture means to hold oneself up against.[1]

When the Body of Christ was redefined according to the world, its connection with the Head was lost. Since some of the visible Body was not connected and functioning according to the Head, it began to lose its sense of identity. After all, the Body can only know its identity by being connected to the Head, Jesus Christ.

Since the connection is being lost in the midst of an unholy mixture, another Jesus can be presented. As the real Jesus is slowly compromised as a means to condition the people into complying with the religious box that is being presented, these people are brought under the influence of another spirit. This spirit will be an extension of the worldly spirit in operation, but it will be clothed in religion, thereby, being capable of becoming a religious substitute for Jesus.

Hence enters the affront against the true Gospel of Jesus Christ. The Gospel of Jesus is the power of God unto salvation. Although it is simple enough for a child to embrace, it has been clearly ordained by heaven. As the Church of Jesus, believers have been commissioned to preach this message.[2] Note that, as Christians we are to preach it, not devise methods by which we can somehow snatch people out of the kingdom of darkness in order to place them in the kingdom of light. Such activities may be religious and hailed by the organized churches as being successful, but how many are truly saved?

The Gospel is really a place of agreement and exchange. This is why people must receive this message by faith. Each of us must come into agreement with God about our need to be saved from the dictates of sin and its consequences of death upon our souls. This agreement is necessary if we, as believers, are going to exchange our old lives of sin and rebellion for a new life of love, obedience, and service to God.

---

[1] Strong's Exhaustive Concordance of the Bible, #430
[2] Mark 16:15; Romans 1:16; 1 Corinthians 15:1

Such agreement finds it origins at the point of conviction about a person's sin-laden soul in light of the righteousness established by God through Jesus Christ's work of redemption on the cross. This person is able to recognize that, unless their sin is properly dealt with by the work of the cross of Jesus, they will not be able to be placed in Jesus' righteousness wrought by His redemption. Such identification in Jesus' redemption is the only way to avoid the judgment that remains upon those who are still dead and doomed in their spiritual condition.[3]

Although, we may not initially understand all of the implications of this new life upon our salvation, we have indeed become identified with Jesus in His death as the Lamb of God. This identification places us in the grave where all judgment towards our sins is silent, allowing us to realize, by faith, that resurrection power has now been placed within us to bring forth a new life.[4]

The reality of the Gospel is that the message may start out simple, but along the way it has become confusing for many new converts. Receiving the true Gospel ensures salvation. However, those who subtly add to the Gospel complicate the issue of salvation. Such complication opens a person up to another spirit.

When wrong spirits are in operation, they will always subtract or add to the Gospel to take away any real dependency on Christ that establishes a believer on the true foundation. This child-like dependency will also line them up to the real cornerstone. We have seen these subtractions and additions in many different ways. They come by way of association with a particular denomination or adopting certain works.

For example, there are those denominations that claim you must be a member of their particular group to be saved. This is definitely an addition to Jesus' salvation. Even though this particular "church" may purport Christ as Savior, the denomination

---

[3] 1 Corinthians 1:30; 2 Corinthians 5:21
[4] Romans 6:1-10

is subtly claiming the position of Savior, even though it never died for the person.

With these types of denominations purporting to be Savior, then they will either deny the responsibilities Christians have to uphold biblical righteousness in their lives, or they will go to the other extremes where they advocate the works that will identify followers to their particular philosophies.

For example, there is one denomination that states you must be water baptized to be saved. Such claims point to doing some type of works to be saved. However, the Bible states that Jesus alone saves. His salvation is a matter of grace. Granted, such works as water baptism will be a natural, but it will also be an upright response or extension of salvation, but such works are not a prerequisite of it. After all, we are condemned because we do not believe the Gospel, not because we fail to be baptized.[5]

This brings us to the next stage of the breakdown. Now that Jesus has been compromised, and there is another spirit in operation, promoting its own lifeless religion, the Gospel will be cleverly perverted without too much opposition from those who are being influenced by the heretical presentation.

The Apostle Paul talked about the seriousness behind presenting another or perverted Gospel. Those who are foolish enough to do it already stand cursed and will face greater damnation.[6] It is important to understand that all you have to do to pervert the Gospel is to take away from it or add to it. When you take away from the Gospel, you are watering it down in some way, rendering it powerless. If you are adding to it, you are stripping it of its simplicity and the power to save. In both cases the intent or spirit of the Gospel has been changed.[7]

---

[5] Mark 16:15-16; Ephesians 2:8-10
[6] Galatians 1:6-9
[7] If you want an in-depth understanding of how the Gospel has been perverted, see the author's book, *The Presentation of the Gospel* in volume 5 of the Foundation Series.

As I read the works of some of the late, great servants of God, the one element I am aware of is how they maintained the integrity of the Gospel. In fact, their presentation of the Gospel has put life into my spirit. It stirs me up to once again consecrate my life. It feeds my soul with a greater sense of who my precious Lord is, and what His redemption means for my life.

In considering some of the popular works of the authors of today, all I can say is that if they do present the Gospel at all, it is so watered down that it has no life or meat to it. It may appeal to my sentiment or pride, but it leaves me empty. In fact, most presentations I have heard sound like flimsy attempts to justify any association or use of Jesus' name because there is no heart or spirit behind it.

My question is simple, "Whatever happened to the Gospel of Jesus Christ?" When did the intent of the Gospel change? As already pointed out, the simplicity of the Gospel has been changed or complicated by the various subtractions and additions of religion. When you change or complicate the simplicity of the Gospel, you are going to frustrate the grace of God. In other words, you are going to make its very work in your life void.

God's grace makes one statement—that salvation is God showing favor towards man so that he can receive His eternal life. This favor allows man to do right towards God, but such deeds will not make him acceptable to God. Rather, they will simply serve as an extension of, or as evidence that eternal life is present, as well as being established in him.[8]

However, the real problem with the false gospels that are being presented is that there is no life in any of them. In other words, the Holy Spirit is not in them. The Gospel is powerful because of the preparation that is done by the Spirit of God to receive it. He is the one who anoints the vessel that proclaims this simple message. This anointing is what is going to impact the souls of others. He is

---

[8] Romans 3:23; 6:23; Galatians 2:21; Ephesians 2:8-10

also the one who prepares people to receive the truth of the Gospel with the conviction of sin, righteousness, and judgment.[9]

In fact, when the Holy Spirit has been present in the presentation of the Gospel, I have witnessed people literally running forward to get matters right with God. There was no need to try to stir people up intellectually or emotionally to compel them to come forward. The Spirit had already laid upon their sin-laden souls the need to do business with God.

There are reasons that the Spirit is missing from much of the evangelistic methods that have been implemented to present the Gospel. The first one is obvious. Any subtraction or addition to the Gospel creates an unholy mixture that the Spirit will not honor. When there is an unholy mixture in regard to the Gospel, the light of the Gospel will be compromised, causing it to become dim. The light of the Gospel is Jesus Christ.[10] When one compromises who He is, the person will strip the Gospel of its power to penetrate the heart.

If the Holy Spirit and the light of Jesus are missing, then there will be a void that must be filled with man's best attempts to get people to give some type of an appearance that salvation is taking place. Obviously, the true Gospel has been replaced with methods that con, logic, plead, or manipulate the person to say some type of prayer of salvation.

These methods may appeal to the intellect or the emotions, but they often fail to penetrate down to the spirit of man to awaken him to his dreadful condition of sin and death. In a way, man is responding to the message from the premise of his own darkness of self-delusion and not from the urgency of seeing the need to get things right with a holy God who will one day cease to be longsuffering towards the influence, workings, and activities of sin

---

[9] John 16:7-11
[10] 2 Corinthians 4:3-6

in his life.[11] Keep in mind that man's darkness will never come into agreement with the light of the Gospel. It is only when the light of the Gospel penetrates the darkness of a person's soul that they will see the desperate need to seek God's forgiveness, redemption, and reconciliation at the cross of Christ.

The light of Jesus is meant to bring a contrast to our spiritual condition. As you study John the Baptist who prepared the way for the Messiah, the light of the world, you realize that people must first be prepared to receive the Gospel. Such preparation comes with the call to repentance so that sins can be remitted or pardoned by God.[12]

If people are going to come to the wells of salvation, they need to be aware that they have a sin problem that must be rectified. This will take the conviction of the Holy Spirit. Therefore, the Holy Spirit convicts of sin, bringing about godly repentance that will cause a person to turn from such sin to receive the gift of life. Once a person repents, then they must be converted to the ways of righteousness. It is not enough to turn from old ways unless they are ready to be converted by the new ways of righteousness.

I can remember my salvation experience. Months before I received the gift of Jesus' life, I was being prepared to repent. The light of the Gospel began to penetrate my dark, foreboding soul with the reality of my sin. The Holy Spirit allowed me to feel the weight of my sin upon my soul. The weight became so great that a cloud of depression was consuming me. I suspected that God was an answer to my problem, but my understanding of Him was vague; therefore, He appeared indifferent and far away.

Through a series of events, the Lord led me to some real Christians who knew the solution to my sin problem. The first time some committed Christian women shared Jesus with me, I was so much stirred in my spirit that I even asked her to take me to her

---

[11] 2 Peter 3:9
[12] Mark 1:4, 15; Luke 13:3, 5

church. God's presence and power met me when I entered the doors of their local church. To this day I cannot tell you the message that was delivered during the services, but I can tell you the overwhelming revelation of His love that I experienced.

God's love for me was gently drawing me to the reality of the salvation He had so freely provided for me. I received the loving revelation of His Son's death on the cross as my solution to my sin. When I walked out of that church, the burden of my sin had rolled away. I walked away with a living witness in my heart that I had indeed been delivered from the entanglements of sin and the consequences of eternal separation from God.

When the Gospel message presented is watered down because it is missing the revelation of sin, then a person will not understand what they are being saved from.[13] As a result, you have people who have a false hope of being saved from a bad life, unpleasant situations, financial difficulties, or despair, but not from sin. If the person is not being saved from sin, then they will fail to understand what they are being saved unto.

Salvation is not just a matter of being delivered from sin and death, but it is also about being delivered into a whole new life where one can actually experience the glorious reality of God in a living relationship. Since the Gospel is being watered down in one aspect, it will possess a different emphasis.

For example, people who accept these watered-down gospels can perceive that they are being delivered into the life they so desire. Hence enter gospels that are influenced by worldly philosophies. They will socialize you, judaize you, entertain you, and make you feel good about yourself, but they will not save you. There is no place of real agreement between God and the person who possesses such a gospel that will result in true reconciliation.

---

[13] If you would like to understand the influence, workings and activities of sin upon your life, see the author's book, *The Anatomy of Sin* in Volume 1 of the Foundation Series.

Since the emphasis of these false gospels is wrong, the churches that promote them often become nothing more than religious social clubs.

It is also important to point out that, when you make Christianity a religious activity or a matter of doctrine, rather than a life, Jesus will be rendered into some type of controllable intellectual concept. When people are encouraged, manipulated, or emotionally twisted like pretzels to <u>accept</u> Jesus as their Savior, it seems like a logical or sentimental thing to do. However, Jesus is a Living Person who needs to be <u>received</u> into the heart as Lord and Savior. [14]

Although you can interchange the two words "accept" and "receive", they can have different emphasis behind them. This is why the King James Version of the Bible uses the word "receive" when it comes to our life in Christ.

Intellectually, I can accept any type of concept about Jesus that is cleverly or emotionally presented. However, to receive the life of Christ entails faith that actually believes the Gospel is true and receives His very promise of life as a reality in the heart. The Bible is clear that salvation is a heart revelation and not an intellectual assent. We are born again in the spirit or inner being, not born again in our minds or at the point of our intellects. It is only as our spirit is born again that our mind can begin to be transformed by the life of the Spirit working within our inner man to receive the fullness of God. [15]

When you water down what it means to receive Jesus, people will fail to recognize that the Gospel is not just about understanding a matter, but having a complete change that will manifest itself in a new life. If that new life is not being made evident, a person must examine whether or not they received Jesus.

---

[14] John 1:12
[15] John 3:3, 5; Romans 10:9-10; Romans 12:2

The one abiding truth I have been aware of is that it is the Godhead who saves. The Father draws people to His Son, while the Son invites people to come to Him as their Lord and Savior in order to drink of the water that will spring up into everlasting life. The Holy Spirit convicts people of their need to be saved from their sin and God's judgment, unto the righteousness of Jesus.[16]

Since God is the one who saves, He moves in spite of, around, and sometimes through man's different methods and attempts to draw people to the Gospel. In essence, God is always quick to honor the tender heart that truly is seeking some type of solution, in spite of the lifeless and religious attempts of man.

This awareness of God's faithfulness to save even those who might not even realize He is looking for them shows not only His power to save, but also His commitment to save. It is not His will that any of us perish in our sins. He has provided the means by which to save each of us from our dreadful plight. In light of this sobering truth, I am also very much aware that the righteous are scarcely saved.[17]

It is impossible to save ourselves, and God must penetrate our hard hearts of arrogance and unbelief to show us our need for His salvation. It is God's longsuffering that allows for the time of preparation that results in godly repentance. It is His mercy that refrains from judging us in our doomed state of sin and death. It also is His grace that is quick to show us favor in our undeserving state by giving us eternal life. This is the glorious reality, assurance, and hope of the Gospel.

There is only one question left, have you truly received the revelation of the Gospel in your heart? Has the issue of your sin been properly dealt with? Does the revelation of the Gospel continue to change your life? Only you can answer these questions. Remember, salvation is a work of God, but you must

---

[16] Luke 9:56; John 4:13-14; 6:44; 7:37-39; 16:8-11
[17] 1 Peter 4:17-18; 2 Peter 3:9

receive by faith every aspect of the Gospel message as being true to ensure you have received eternal life.

10

REPROBATE FAITH

We have been considering how the influence of the world has affected the face of the professing Church. Obviously, the only thing the world can do for the Church is to defile it by changing its identity. It has simply been conformed to a religious image that has no life or substance behind it.

As we follow the digression of the professing Church into its present state, we can see how its concept of its identity would change according to the world's influence. The foundation has been redefined, the cornerstone readjusted, and the Gospel perverted to conform it to the various images that have been set forth by man and the world.

Sadly, if believers do not seek the true Church's identity in Scripture, they will become confused by what is nothing more than a worldly presentation. After all, as they look at these different worldly presentations of the Church, it is almost like looking at a mirror, but the mirror has been broken. Although the glass has been put back together by the best attempts of man, it still is perverted. In its overall presentation, this mirror is riddled with cracks that break the continuity of the presentation. In other places, it is fragmented where it fails to make sense, and clouded due to abuse and neglect. Therefore, there is no real clear image or presentation of the Church when it comes to the world.

The only place the Church can gain its real identity is from looking at itself through the eyes of the Jesus of the Bible. He is the foundation, the cornerstone, and the only light in the Gospel. He is the one that died on the cross for His Body. As a result, the members of His Body have been seated in high places with Him.[1]

Clearly, believers' vantage point will not be earthbound, world-inspired, or man-manipulated. It will be a heavenly vantage point that will keep believers far above the entanglements of the world and the limited, useless attempts of man.

This brings us to the final breakdown of the life of the professing Church. There are what I consider to be sad statements or sayings in the Bible. Every time I come to one of these sayings, my heart is wrenched at the prospect of what is being said. In these sayings, there is sadness, as well as urgency. Most of these statements come in the form of a question. A question calls for personal examination.

For example, the first sad statement in the Bible is found in *Genesis 3:9, "And the LORD God called unto Adam, and said unto him. Where art thou?"* God knew where Adam was, but Adam had to face that the fellowship between his Creator and him had been broken by his disobedience in the garden. Instead of man walking with God, he would now hide from God as he attempted to cover up the guilt of his sin behind worldly fig leaves of shame and religious cloaks of self-righteousness.[2]

Jesus also made some sad statements to His disciples. Every time I read these statements my heart becomes sorrowful. In fact, I can almost see Him saying it to me when the times are tough or I am giving way to the old man.

One of these statements was made after many of His followers turned back to their old ways to never follow Him again. For Adam, he broke fellowship with God, but for Jesus' disciples, His truth

---

[1] Ephesians 2:6
[2] John 15:22

insulted them. Since they could not understand the truth Jesus spoke, they became uncertain and judgmental towards Him, and departed. These followers did not realize that the sharpness of Jesus' truths would not only expose their level of dedication, but their motives. Obviously, they were not totally consecrated to serving Him. It was at this time that Jesus asked this penetrating question of His remaining disciples in *John 6:67b, "Will ye also go away?"*

Jesus asked another sad question that always makes me stop and ponder the warning and urgency of it. It is found in *Luke 18:8b: "Nevertheless, when the Son of man cometh, shall he find faith on the earth?"*

As you consider the digression of the presentation of the Church due to its union with the world, it is obvious that all matters relating to the kingdom of God have been redefined, readjusted, perverted, and undermined. The pure has been defiled, truth compromised, integrity sacrificed, and true consecration mocked. The Apostle Paul summarized the state of affairs when he made this statement in *Titus 1:15-16,*

> *Unto the pure all things are pure, but unto them that are defiled and unbelieving is nothing pure; but even their mind and conscience is defiled. They profess that they know God, but in works they deny him, being abominable, and disobedient, and unto every good work reprobate.*

"Reprobate" is an interesting word. It means unapproved, rejected, worthless, and a castaway.[3] When you study this word, you will realize that something is being cast off or rejected because it is impure. It is not coming from an acceptable origin or premise. In each case, it is coming from something that has already been defiled. In *Titus*, we see that even good works will be rejected if they come from a wrong premise.

---

[3] Strong's Exhaustive Concordance of the Bible; #96

The Apostle Paul also spoke of a reprobate mind in *Romans 1:28.* We know that we have all been given an inward sense that there is a God. This sense also gives us a semblance of His character.[4] Granted, we may not personally know Him, and we may even refuse to listen to that inner sense, ultimately rejecting that aspect of our conscience altogether. But, on judgment day, there will be no excuse for us not really coming to terms with the true God of heaven.

The Apostle Paul described how people acquire a reprobate mind. First, they refuse to glorify God in their lives. The reason for this is because they are unthankful and caught up with their vain imaginations. These imaginations begin to darken their already foolish hearts with greater delusion. In other words, the foolish heart will justify its wicked attitude. Such an attitude will begin to change the glory of God as it gives way to its idolatrous pursuits and preferences.[5]

As the person gives way to their idolatrous ways, God will give them over to the lusts of their own heart. This is a form of judgment where such individuals will experience the emptiness and bitterness of these useless pursuits, as well as consequences. It also means that their deceitful and rebellious heart will manifest itself in unclean practices as they begin to dishonor their bodies.[6]

Dishonoring one's body clearly points to fornication, which involves coming into agreement with the unholy in some way. The Apostle Paul made reference to this in *1 Corinthians 6:18, "Flee fornication. Every sin that a man doeth is without the body; but he that committeth fornication sinneth against his own body."*

In this unholy agreement, the person will exchange the truth of God for a lie as they begin to worship and serve their lusts, pursuits, and/or unholy unions. As these individuals are given over

---

[4] Romans 1:18-20
[5] Romans 1:21-23
[6] Romans 1:24

111

to their wicked master, God will give them up to pursue their vile affections, as even the natural becomes inordinate. It is from this premise that God will give these people over to a reprobate mind that no longer retains any real knowledge of Him.[7]

As we consider the word "reprobate" in the text of a reprobate mind, we can see that a mind that does not retain the knowledge of the true God is worthless. However, remember this mind gave up any real desire to know the true God. It preferred its inordinate lusts and wicked pursuits to honoring the true God of heaven. Therefore, we can see where our minds and our good works can be considered reprobate or useless because of their source or motivation.

This brings us to something else that can also be considered worthless because of its source or motivation. Heed the apostle's words, *"Examine yourselves, whether you are in the faith; prove yourselves. Know ye not yourselves how Jesus Christ is in you, except ye be reprobate" (2 Corinthians 13:5)*.

The Apostle Paul stated that we, as Christians, could be considered worthless or castaways. This was one of the Apostle Paul's personal concerns as well. He made this statement, *"But I keep under my body, and bring it into subjection, lest that by any means, when I have preached to others, I myself should be a castaway" (1 Corinthians 9:27)*. In *2 Corinthians 13:5*, the Apostle Paul brought out that the test of our worth will be based on whether we are in the true faith.

In the last three decades, I have seen the presentation of faith change many times. Today, much of the faith that is being presented is unscriptural and worthless. For me, the big struggle has been to come to terms with genuine faith.[8] After all, there is only one true faith. It was clearly first delivered to the saints. This

---

[7] Romans 1:26-28

[8] If you would like to know about what the author discovered about faith, see her book titled, *In Search of Real Faith*.

faith has not changed; therefore, there are no new revelations concerning it. In fact, we are told to contend for the faith that was first delivered to the saints.[9] "Contend" means to struggle for something in order to maintain a proper grip on it.[10] It could be related to a wrestling match.

There are so many pseudo faiths that have blown through Christendom. Sadly, I have watched people being swept away by these ridiculous winds.[11] However, the Bible is clear about what constitutes genuine faith. To make sure we start from the right premise, we must understand what faith is.

To describe "faith," words such as believe, persuasion, conviction, trust, assurance, and faithfulness are used. Faith involves a choice of the will. I must choose to **believe** a matter is true. The reason I choose to believe a matter is true is because I am **persuaded** by a sincere **conviction**. This conviction will cause me to put my *confidence or trust* in it. I will be able to be **assured** about my confidence because the character of **faithfulness** is clearly present to confirm my trust.

This brings me to the first issue of my faith. What must I choose to believe to be true? *Romans 10:17* gives me the bases on which our confidence or trust as believers will begin. *"So, then, faith cometh by hearing, and hearing by the word of God."* The source of any believer's faith is founded on what the Word of God says. Why is the Word of God so important? It is a record of who God is and His dealings with man. We must choose to believe that God's Word is true and faithful in order to embrace its testimonies.

All unbelief in a person's life begins at the same point. They justify away, ignore, or refuse to believe the Word of God about a matter, thereby, failing to obey it. *Romans 14:23b* tells us that whatsoever does not originate from or respond according to

---

[9] Ephesians 4:5; Jude 3
[10] Strong's Exhaustive Concordance of the Bible, #1864
[11] Ephesians 4:14

113

genuine faith will be considered sin. When King David was confronted by the prophet Nathan concerning his sins of adultery and murder, this statement was made, *"Wherefore hast thou despised the commandment of the LORD, to do evil in his sight...?" (2 Samuel 12:9a).*

King David was the man that expounded on the need and importance of loving the commandments of God, and yet he failed to believe and apply them to his own life when he found himself in temptation and sin. In fact, once he fell into the cesspool of sin, his deeds led to the murder of one of his devoted soldiers. God said of David's actions that they showed that he was actually despising, disesteeming, disdaining, or scorning His commandments at that point in his life.[12]

Sadly, the authority and power of God's Word has been replaced by man's traditions and religious activities that include such things as good works and coming back under the covenant of the Old Testament Law.

Instead of the Word being used to discern a matter, it is often interpreted according to the doctrine or theology of man. Therefore, it is adjusted to fit man's personal understanding or preference towards a spiritual truth or issue. The key to true faith is that it approaches the Word to believe it, not to debate or adjust it according to personal preferences, understanding, or doctrine. The world will defile the things of God, but man always perverts it. He is forever adding to it or taking away from it.

Faith comes down to where we are putting our reliance or confidence. In many cases, man is putting his faith in what he understands or perceives about God. This type of individual actually perceives and professes themselves as being wise, but the reality is that they are foolish for putting their confidence in that which has no spirit or truth. Such a premise is nothing more than perversion. In fact, it is a way to frustrate the grace of God

---

[12] Strong's Exhaustive Concordance of the Bible, #959

because such individuals are failing to recognize the complete work of redemption that was accomplished on the cross. As the Apostle Paul declared in *Romans 5:21, "That as sin hath reigned unto death, even so might grace reign through righteousness unto eternal life by Jesus Christ, our Lord."* Once again, as believers, we are reminded that faith is reckoned or counted to us for righteousness.[13]

One of the most blatant examples of this perversion can be found among those who do not believe Jesus is God in the flesh. They have come to this conclusion based on their own vain, perverted, and logical evaluation and/or on information that has been twisted to fit their conclusions. As a result, they have changed the glory of God that was manifested in the flesh and made Him into a mere man that did a sacrificial deed. Obviously, these people do not believe the record given concerning Jesus Christ. They clearly have not approached the Bible to believe it; rather, they have approached it to debate, refute, and reject whatever does not fit into their perverted concept about Jesus Christ.

Faith entails being persuaded that something is legitimate. In other words, we, as believers, are being persuaded that the Word of God is truth. The Apostle Paul clearly brings this out in *2 Timothy 1:12, "For which cause I also suffer these things; nevertheless, I am not ashamed; for I know whom I have believed and am persuaded that he is able to keep that which I have committed unto him against that day."*

One of the fruits I have grown to appreciate about genuine faith is that it enables me to face reality. There is not much I like about the reality that constantly confronts me. Over the years, I have discovered that the source of my confidence is going to

---

[13] Romans 1:22; 4:9; Galatians 2:21

determine how I confront the many issues of life.[14] These issues can include such unpleasant challenges as bothersome troubles, losses, and death.

Genuine faith strictly finds its source in God. One of the principle doctrines of Christ is faith towards God. Notice, genuine faith is directed at God. Scriptures clearly reveals to us that we are identified to the spiritual seed of Abraham based on this faith.

It is this faith that also identifies us to the great cloud of witness mentioned in *Hebrews 12:1*. We are told that we are given a measure of faith.[15] This measure of faith allows us to take steps of obedience in light of who God is.

When you consider the faith of many in the professing Church, their confidence is not in God. The main push behind their misdirected faith is not to walk by faith through the trials of life in confidence of God; rather, it is a means to change their reality so that they do not have to be tested in the fiery ovens of adversity.[16]

For some, they have put their confidence in their words. They try to change reality by claiming or professing their desired reality. Such words lack truth and spirit; therefore, they are idle words. The intent behind such words is selfish and has nothing to do with the will of God. Such words will reveal the treasures that are truly being valued in these people's hearts. Jesus made this statement about idle words in *Matthew 12:35-47*,

> *A good man out of the good treasure of the heart bringeth forth good things, and an evil man out of the evil treasure bringeth forth evil things. But I say unto you that every idle word that men shall speak, they shall give account of it in the day of judgment. For by thy words thou shalt be justified, and by thy words thou shalt be condemned.*

---

[14] If you would like to understand the real matters affecting life, see the author's book, *The Issues of Life* in volume 5 of the Foundation Series.

[15] Romans 12:3; Galatians 3:6-9; Hebrews 6:1

[16] 2 Corinthians 5:7; 1 Peter 1:6-8

Some of these individuals even use God's promises to try to get their way in their particular realities. It is as though they take His promises and beat Him over the head with them until they are fulfilled according to their perspective. However, *Hebrews 6:12* gives us this insight about God's promises, *"That ye be not slothful, but followers of them who though faith and patience inherit the promises."*

Christians who truly understand faith recognize that their faith does not possess any power. Regardless of the methods that are used, faith cannot move God's arm if the prayer, pursuit, or desire is contrary to His character, will, and timing. Therefore, faith does not move God; rather, it personally moves and inspires the believer in confidence, as well as with conviction and diligence, to faithfully believe and obey the Lord until the conditions of the promises are fulfilled.[17]

The main desire of faith is to seek God out in order to do His will. It desires to please God in all that it does. Once faith responds in the proper way, God is able to meet the believer and count their action for righteousness. Clearly, genuine faith simply allows God to be God. Genuine faith is often accredited with moving mountains, but, in reality, it allows God the correct environment to move obstacles. Clearly, God desires to confirm and honor genuine faith by doing the miraculous in the lives of His faithful servants.[18]

Faith clearly comes down to a person's real point of confidence. This is why we are told that we cannot please God without faith.[19] Faith chooses to trust God, not according to His power, but according to His character. Faith knows that God does not lie and that He is faithful to those who are His. Even in the darkest time of his life, Job chose to put trust and assurance in

---

[17] James 2:23-26
[18] Matthew 17:20; Romans 3:28; 4:3; Hebrews 11:6; James 5:16: 1 John 5:14
[19] Hebrews 11:6

God's character and not in his circumstances. His statement confirmed his abiding assurance that he had towards God in *Job13:15, "Though he slay me, yet will I trust in him; but I will maintain mine own ways before him."* Even if God required his very life, Job would not only trust Him, but he understood that he would be able to maintain or defend his ways before God because they were a matter of sincere faith towards Him.

This brings us back to where people put their reliance. The confusion rests with the fact that people put their reliance on religious things, but it is not in God. They can put their reliance in their denominations, theologies, good works, and religious activities, but all of these pseudo faiths are simply putting confidence in the arm of man. The prophet, Jeremiah had some strong words about such misplaced confidence,

> *Thus saith the LORD, Cursed be the man that trusteth in man, and maketh flesh his arm, and whose heart departeth from the LORD. For he shall be like the heath in the desert, and shall not see when good cometh, but shall inhabit the parched places in the wilderness, in a salt land and not inhabited. Blessed is the man who trusteth in the LORD, and whose hope the LORD is. (Jeremiah 17:5-7)*

Clearly, there is only one place where we can put our confidence, and that is our Lord Jesus Christ. This brings us back to the warning of the Apostle Paul. If our faith is not in the Lord Jesus Christ of the Bible, we will prove to be reprobates in our Christian life. Therefore, if people's scriptural understanding about spiritual matters is not founded on the Person of Jesus, God will reject them as the storms of life expose the fallacy of their foundation. If their conduct does not line up to Jesus as the cornerstone, they will find their ways and works counted as worthless before God. If they are not properly identified to the Head, they will be considered castaways.

For the last twenty centuries, the true Church has had to wade through the many different pseudo faiths that have taken center stage. However, the real Church is able to identify the faith that was first delivered to the saints because it has been clearly unveiled in Scripture. God would never expect us to possess the true faith if He had not outlined it through instructions and examples.

As you study the lives of those found in *Hebrews 11*, you realize they make up a great cloud of witnesses. These witnesses show us that walking by faith is not only possible, but also rewarding. In fact, this walk serves as the most natural expression of those who truly love God and want to please Him.

As you study this chapter in Hebrews, you can see where active faith inspired these people to risk it all to discover God. They were all seeking God. Abraham not only understood that God was his portion, but he sought the city made by God. In faith towards God's instructions, Noah built an ark, even though he had never seen the rain. Moses refused to enjoy sin for a season so he could be identified with God's people. There were those who sought a better resurrection, regardless of the cost, and there were still others whose faith the world was not even worthy to witness. Truly, these people's faith brought such pleasure to God that He would not share it with an age that would surely mock it.

This brings us to a very important aspect of a life of unfeigned faith. Such a walk is what will bring us into discovering the fullness and majesty of God. Such fullness points to complete satisfaction. Today, people, including professing Christians, are trying to fill the empty vacuum in their souls with activities and things or stuff from the world. Although such things may bring a temporary satisfaction, such satisfaction will not last. As a result, such people move on to other pursuits.

For the Christian who discovers the life that the great cloud of witnesses speaks of, they have also discovered the satisfaction that will fill and maintain the soul. It is the life of Christ in each of us, as Christians, that must fill every aspect of our lives with a sense of revelation, awe, and worship. As Scripture states about Jesus, *"For in him dwelleth all the fullness of the Godhead bodily...Where there is neither Greek nor Jew, circumcision nor uncircumcision, barbarian, Scythian, bond nor free, but Christ is all, and in all" (Colossians 2:9; 3:11).*

The fullness of Christ is the life that unfeigned faith will discover in its walk. It is complete and worth all that it may cost each of us to secure it.

For Abraham, it gave him a perspective that reached beyond his present age into eternity. For Noah, it gave him an ark that delivered him through the judgment upon the present age of his day. For Moses, it gave him a point of identification, even in the midst of great slavery to endure the age of great testing in the wilderness. In essence, faith allows saints to discover God in the barren wilderness of the darkness of their present age.

What about your faith or point of reliance? Is it in what you think you know? Perhaps it is in what you do for God? Maybe your point of reliance is in your particular denomination or words or even in using God's promises to get your way concerning the things of this present age? Maybe you think that, by coming back under the Old Testament Law (the deeds and doctrine of the Nicolaitans), it is going to earn God's approval?

However, if your faith is not in the true God of the Bible and His provision of Jesus Christ, your whole life could be considered reprobate before Him. What a waste! As believers, we must remember, that on the great day of judgment when all will be stripped from each of us, only the pure gold of unfeigned faith, the refined silver of redemption that has been tried in the fires of testing and separation, and the precious stones of our loving devotion will survive the penetrating fire of His holy judgment upon all of that which has been truly committed to Him by faith.[20]

---

[20] 1 Corinthians 3:12-15; 1 Peter 1:6-9

Part III

THE POWERLESS PULPIT

11

THE PURPOSE

We have considered how the Church has been influenced by the world and how a shift has taken place in the leadership. As a result, the sheep are scattering in every direction in attempts to find waters (preaching and teaching) that have not been muddied with some type of heretical poisons, as well as pastures (fellowships) that are free from the attack of predators. They are seeking shepherds who truly possess the heart of Jesus.

There clearly has been a strong undercurrent that has been moving the visible Church away from the center of the Rock. Obviously, different congregations have been boxed in by man's religions, dulled down by worldly influences, and experienced a shift from Christ-centered leadership to man-centered rule. As a result, these local bodies are also witnessing what I refer to as the "powerless pulpit." A "powerless pulpit" is a pulpit that has no means by which to impact people's lives. Without the right impact flowing from the pulpits, an identity crisis can erupt in those who are part of these congregations. These individuals will actually feel disconnected and confused about their lives in Christ.

There are a couple of reasons why pulpits are proving to be powerless in churches. The first reason is that congregations are not prepared or opened to any spiritual revolution that could be created by a pulpit that is aflame with the power of God. Many of these individuals in such congregations still find their identification with the world and not in the Jesus of the Bible. Some have been conditioned by heretical presentations and have been indoctrinated by man in some way. As a result, these individuals have not really accepted the call of Jesus to become His disciples. Because of this unreceptive attitude of those who sometimes represent the majority in certain congregations, pastors who could bring life back to the pulpit are passed over, disregarded, or shunned.

The second reason has to do with those who hold the title or position of a pastor. Many have given way to or fallen prey to the compromising, worldly, and heretical environment and philosophies that are invading much of the visible Church. Such pastors are nothing more than the "walking dead." They have no flame of inspiration (fire from the throne), light (resurrection life), or heavenly perspective to pass on the torch that has been entrusted to the true Church of Jesus. Therefore, dulled down, lifeless congregations and "dead" pastors are being drawn together, creating a dangerous scenario for those who innocently find themselves in such an environment.

As you consider this environment, you will realize that it enables people to *play* Church rather than become *part* of the living Church, Body, or extension of Jesus Christ. The other aspect of this worldly, religious environment is that it makes people feel good about their spiritual conditions. In other words, they actually believe that Jesus came to save them *in* their sin and not *from* it. This type of condition is actually making people feel good in their wretched, condemned state about their compromise with the world, as they merrily continue on their way to hell.

In order to understand the impact that every Christian pulpit should be making, we have to understand what constitutes a "pulpit." This is an important way to address attitudes towards the idea or concept of "pulpit" as a means to come to terms with its purpose.

To understand the purpose of pulpits, we have to consider its meaning. Since pulpits are not mentioned in the Bible, we must look to the secular dictionary to understand the premise of the attitudes that have been developed towards these objects. My dictionary gave a couple of definitions for the word "pulpit."[1]

The first definition is that a pulpit is an elevated platform or high reading desk that is used for preaching or to conduct worship service. Another meaning that the word "pulpit" is associated with is the preaching profession, and, in some cases, it is used to identify a person with a religious position.

As we consider these meanings, we can begin to see the attitude that has been developed towards the concept of the pulpit. First, it is a place of veneration, but whom or what is being exalted? It is a place where something is actually being staged. However, anything that is stage in relationship to God's kingdom often points to activities and schedules that are controlled by man. These elevated places also can point to possible pretense or hypocrisy that has been promoted, encouraged, or condoned through the means of entertainment that has been clearly inspired by the world.

The word "pulpit" is also associated with a profession, but does the presence of the pulpit distinguish the person or does the person define the significance of such a place based on what is being proclaimed from this elevated place? It also points to position. Does a pulpit give a person authority or does the person's authority empower the place of the pulpit?

There was an incident in which a man was asked to inform the congregation of upcoming activities. He was a teacher by profession and admitted that he had secretly longed to stand behind the church's pulpit. However, when he was standing behind the pulpit, informing the congregation of the upcoming activities, he felt intimidated by it. He realized that it was not just a

---

[1] Webster's Dictionary

matter of standing behind it, but of being equipped to actually fulfill the actual purpose for which it was designated.

In dealing with the issues of the pulpit, I have noticed a pulpit has no real meaning other than what people associate with it. Pulpits vary in sizes, looks, and presentations. Mere man may stand behind these objects, but, otherwise, it stands silent most of the time.

It is clear that the pulpit has no purpose outside of simply serving as a stand on which information can be placed. This stand, in many cases, has been elevated so the crowds or masses can see the speakers. Take away the pulpit and the stage, and the person who was elevated will once again be placed on equal footing with everyone else. This shows us that the real importance of the pulpit does not necessarily rest with the one who is speaking.

This brings us to the information or messages, which can include songs, that are being delivered from the pulpit. The purpose of the pulpit is to share, proclaim, or bring forth some kind of message. Clearly, people are not there to watch an individual simply stand behind a pulpit, rather they are present to hear what a person has to say in regard to a subject or matter. In summation, they are there to hear the message.

Sadly, man has been improperly exalted above the message, drowning out the real purpose for a pulpit. Consider for a moment, if people are present to simply venerate a man behind the pulpit instead of hearing the message, they are basically wasting their time. Granted the validity of man will be tested and established by his message, but the impact of the message will hinge on whether man has the necessary authority to deliver it. Therefore, the real purpose of a pulpit is to deliver an important message that will prove to be viable to the lives of others.

As I have stood behind different pulpits to share a message in regard to my faith, I have regarded them as altars, tables, or a place of exaltation. For example, it is from the altar of the pulpit that preachers or speakers offer up some type of sacrifice to God. These sacrifices must be holy to be considered acceptable to God. Acceptable sacrifices will emit some type of fragrance that will prove to be well-pleasing to God, bringing Him glory.

To me, a pulpit is a table of showbread. At this table, the bread of the Word will be broken and presented as food to sustain the inner lives of those who are present. For some, the bread must be dissolved into the milk of pure doctrine for them to drink of it. For others, it must be presented with the meat of righteousness to ensure maturity. Such impartation can prove challenging to any messenger, but the main goal of the messenger is to ensure that such priceless food is not flung at the people, but that it is actually being imparted to them.

This brings us to whom or what needs to be exalted from the Christian pulpit. There is only One person who deserves to be exalted from the pulpits of the churches that has His name associated with them, and that is the Lord Jesus Christ. It is His Gospel that must be proclaimed. He is the bread from heaven that must be properly imparted into the lives of His people, and it is the flow of His life that serves as a sweet savor to God.[2] It is from such a pulpit that man ceases to be the center of attention, as the message is empowered, and the people impacted.

When we consider what the real purpose of the pulpit is, we must examine why it has become powerless. Perhaps it is obvious to some. Instead of offering sacrifices that are pleasing to God, there are those who use the pulpit to offer up profane offerings to God that are emitting a stench to Him. Rather, than imparting the Word to feed the souls of people, leaders are feeding the people's minds with a mixture of worldly philosophies, such as psychology, along with what I consider to be nothing more than Biblical notions.

---

[2] John 6:35; 12:32; 2 Corinthians 2:15-16; Hebrews 5:11-14

Biblical notions are when man takes a subject out of the Bible and adjusts it to his own self-serving preference. One such preference is the notion that God's whole goal is to see man happy, enriched with the world's goods, and pursuing that which is pleasing to him. Such a notion is man-centered, which makes it humanistic to the core. To offer this type of combination to God would be the same as offering strange fire to Him. Such fire resulted in the death of Aaron's sons and, sadly, is resulting in a tidal wave of destruction that will take many unsuspecting people into judgment.

Obviously, to offer unacceptable mixtures from the pulpits would render such pulpits powerless. In such cases, the preacher simply becomes an entertainer, and the message becomes nothing more than fluff that contains the residues of poison and death for those who partake of it.

Are there any pulpits in your life? Take time to examine them to see what kind of offering is being made by the leaders. If the strange or profane is being offered to God, flee from such a place for the wrath of God will be abiding on such a pulpit.

12

THE PLACE OF WITNESS

When people stray from the center after finding themselves in an identity crisis, they begin to struggle to bring back some order, meaning, and purpose in their lives. In their desperate attempts, they often jump on the pendulum that is now beginning to swing from side to side in regard to the issues that have caused a tidal wave of confusion.

Cleary, the pendulum is swinging in Christendom. Those who try to gauge which side of the pendulum they want to associate with find themselves being flung into extremes. Even truth that is taken into any extreme becomes a point of deception. After all, God does not deal in extremes, but operates from the center of what is true, pure, and just. Center points to balance, not chaos, sanity rather than ridiculousness, and clarity instead of confusion.

Obviously, the sane action to take is to avoid the pendulum that is swinging into the extreme areas of religion and come back to center in order to establish what is sound. The prophet Haggai in the first chapter actually instructed the people of Israel two times to consider their ways. According to the *Strong's Exhaustive Concordance,* "consider" in this text pointed to coming back to center in order to establish the acceptable and right order.

As the problem in the visible Church gains the momentum of a tsunami, the debate rages on among those who are trying to bring some type of semblance to the Church before the momentum causes many to become shipwrecked in their faith. But such attempts result in some of these well-meaning people desperately snatching at straws that have already been flung up in the air by the present winds of judgment.

It does appear as if a great dam of destruction has broken, and its waters are sweeping many away from the sanity and safety of truth. However, the key is not to stop the flow of waters, for they will come, but to properly identify and address the breach that has been made through apparent compromise and neglect. No doubt, there could be various issues sighted as to the reason for this great breach, but, once again, I would like to weigh in on this matter with my conclusion. Much of the breach has occurred because the pulpit has been rendered powerless.

God has a clear order. This order has been distinguished by clear Scriptural guidelines. In fact, you can actually see God work within these guiding principles. One of the rules that has been brought out through Scripture has to do with witnesses.

A matter can only be confirmed by two or three witnesses.[1] It is not proper to take the word of one witness as being valid. When we consider the concept of one, we realize there is one who is the beginning, fulfillment, and end to all that is trustworthy, and that is God. However, even God confirms a matter with at least three witnesses. Granted, He could rightfully stop with two witnesses, for the number "two" points to agreement, but God usually confirms a matter with three witnesses, which points to the completion or entirety of a matter.

We can see the grouping of these three witnesses in Scripture. In *1 John 5:6-9* we are told there are three that bear record in heaven and three that bear witness in earth. Those who verify the record in heaven are the Father, the Word (Jesus), and the Holy Spirit. Their agreement actually establishes the record that the

---

[1] Deuteronomy 17:6-7; Matthew 18:16

witnesses on earth in turn, will be established as being true. These three witnesses of earth are the Spirit, the water (Word), and the blood of Jesus (covenant). What is the record that is being established and confirmed? *"And this is the record, that God hath given to us eternal life, and this life is in his Son. He that hath the Son hath life; and he that hath not the Son of God hath not life" (1 John 5:11-12).*

There are also three witnesses that confirm the matters of God's existence and character, especially when it comes to His creation, beginning with what has been clearly established in man. There is the witness of the conscience of man that serves as the inner witness that God truly exists. This is why the Apostle Paul warns those who fail to pursue and agree with this witness will end up with a reprobate mind that no longer retains any real knowledge of God.

The second witness of God's existence and His character is creation itself. It allows man to see his Creator's majesty and incredible ways. Because of these two witnesses, man will not be able to hide behind ignorance concerning the existence and character of God. In fact, God will not wink at such ignorance that manifests itself in unbelief; rather, He is commanding men to repent of such darkness to avoid judgment.[2]

Finally, the third witness that confirms God's existence is man himself. Scripture describes man as being nothing more than a clay vessel. However, if the life of Jesus is present in this vessel, man is not only part of the covenant established by the blood of Jesus, but he becomes a living, walking epistle who is read by others.[3] It is through the vessel of man that God verifies the testimony concerning the record of heaven, which must always be in accordance to the witnesses in earth.

---

[2] Acts 17:30-31; Romans 1:18-32
[3] 2 Corinthians 3:2-3; 4:7

This brings us to the three witnesses involved in declaring salvation. As clay vessels, believers possess the life of Christ. It is Jesus' life that is being offered and poured out from these vessels into others. It is the resurrection power associated with this incredible life that serves as the first witness to the work of salvation. The second witness is the seal of the Holy Spirit. It is the power and work of the Spirit that is developing the very life of Christ in believers.

The final witness that God uses to proclaim and verify the matter of salvation is man's voice. A good example of this can be found at Jesus' baptism as recorded in *John 1:15-34.* There were three that verified the record that He was the Son of God. The Father introduced Him as the Son, the Holy Spirit came upon Him to identify Him as the Son of God to the third witness, John the Baptist. It was John who introduced Jesus to others as being the Son of God.

Man is commissioned to testify of, as well as establish, this record through the preaching of the Gospel and through discipling, which is impartation of the Word though such means as teaching.[4] As you consider these three witnesses involving man, it is important to understand that the life of Christ in believers serves as an earthly witness that can be observed by others, the seal of the Spirit as a heavenly witness which points to connection, identity, and power with heaven, and the voice of man as the verbal witness that can be heard by others.

This brings us to the matter of the pulpits that stand in the Christian churches. The reason that so many are powerless is because the necessary witness is missing. Without the witness, nothing will be firmly established in the hearts and minds of God's people. Many will walk away with a vague concept of something, but there will be no clear witness that will bring clarity and revelation to a matter.

---

[4] Matthew 28:18-20; Mark 16:15-16; Galatians 2:20; Ephesians 1:9-14

Why is the necessary witness missing? The reasons vary, but one of the main reasons is that the actual record is missing from much of the preaching and teaching. The purpose of the pulpit is to declare the record that has been firmly established in heaven. The record has to do with the eternal life that can only be obtained through Jesus. This record points to the Gospel which is the power of God onto salvation.

If the record is missing, what does man preach or teach from the pulpits? Sadly, at best, it is a mixture of worldly philosophies and Scriptural doctrine, and, at worst, it is a blatant attack against Scripture. A good example of blatant attack against the Gospel is Social Justice. This gospel substitutes faith toward God with "good works" and replaces righteous judgment with perverted "justice" that penalizes that which is decent, right, and moral.

One of the unholy mixtures in the Church today is what watchmen in the Church refer to as psychobabble. This psychological jargon takes Scriptural principles and institutes them into the philosophy of psychology. When you take an unholy mixture in which self must be esteemed to give a person a good sense of self-worth, you simply make such people feel good about the wretched condition of their lives. As a result, the Gospel is changed from the need to be saved *from* sin to being saved *in* sin. Instead of God being the center of a matter, man is made the center as people take Scriptural truths and try to revolve them around the idol of self.

The record clearly exalts Jesus as God Incarnate. It reveals man needs to be saved from the dictates and consequences of sin. Granted, the cross is about man's need to be saved, but Jesus is being exalted and esteemed on the cross, not man. In fact, the cross shows man he must cease in or die to his old ways in order to take on the very life of Christ. Once a person becomes totally identified with the cross, it ceases to be about them and becomes a matter of the life of Christ being established and brought forth in the person.

If the record is present, but the pulpit remains powerless, it is because the connection with heaven is missing. Jesus never spoke outside of what His Father commanded. In other words, as man, He was connected to the throne of God. He often separated Himself from the crowds to seek the Father in prayer. No doubt, He was receiving inspiration and instruction from the throne.

There is only one means by which believers can truly be connected to heaven, and that is through the Spirit of God. It is the Spirit who guides each of us in all truth.[5] He is the One who inspires and empowers us. However, inspiration of the Spirit comes from the throne, and His power comes only through humility, submission, and obedience.

Some pastors have zeal for God, but lack inspiration. Other pastors have formulas, but lack power. Some of these leaders have a set procedure for how they conduct services, but there is no real humility or sincere dependency (faith) that identifies them to the throne of God. Therefore, pastors or leaders who do not understand how to give way to the Spirit will never have the connection that will identify them to heaven. They are, thereby, rendered ineffective to impact the spirits and souls of men from their pulpits.

This brings me to the subject of preaching and teaching. As the vessel, man's voice simply becomes the means by which God's heart is being proclaimed and presented. Much of the heavenly connection has been taken out of these two presentations because man is either promoting personal agendas or worldly philosophies. He has a mixture where the Word of God is adjusted to fit into the presentation.

These two types of presentations also differ. Preaching stirs up, for it calls for some type of response. For example, the initial

---

[5] John 16:7-13

call in John the Baptist and Jesus' preaching was for people to repent. Inspired teaching from the throne of God does not simply inform us of doctrinal or kingdom matters, but it will challenge us on a personal basis to assimilate the ways of righteousness into our lives through obedience. Both inspired preaching and teaching will bring us to the crossroads of decision as to whether or not we will abandon all to follow Jesus in a sold-out, consecrated life.

Real preaching has almost ceased in some pulpits. Instead of people being stirred up towards God concerning matters of sin, redemption, and eternal life in order to properly respond, they are being pumped up to feel as if they have had some religious experience.

Some people want to feel as if they have been entertained in some sentimental, religious way. Others may see it as a time to catch up on their rest as they are put to sleep by a lifeless message or presentation. However, such exercises speak of the ways of the flesh, and the Holy Spirit will have no part in activities that are clearly being orchestrated by man.

The teaching that is taking place may give some information, but it is directed at the mind, which takes on the form of conceit. Such information has no means by which to transform the mind. It is only revelation brought forth by the Holy Spirit that has the ability to transform the mind. In fact, such revelations come by way of man's spirit with the intent to enlarge his mind to receive the revelation.

Due to the abuses taking place from behind the pulpit, there are some who want to do away with godly responsibilities, such as preaching, to deal with the abuses and problems that are plaguing the visible Church. This would not be dealing with abuses or problems; rather, it would prove to be disobedient. We, as Christians, have been commissioned to preach the Gospel and to disciple (teach) followers of Jesus to observe His Word. Jesus both preached to the crowds and taught them, but He was inspired, empowered, and effective. There was no unholy mixture in what He presented.

It is clear why some pulpits are powerless. Those who stand behind them are failing to maintain the record of heaven through the power of the Spirit, the assimilation of the Word, and the putting on of the godly life wrought by the blood of Jesus.

How about you? Are you exposed to the ineffective work of the "powerless pulpit" or are you becoming established in your own life in Christ? Remember, it is *your* life in Christ.

13

THE SWORD

We have been considering the "powerless pulpit." Obviously, it is the record or message that is being delivered that will determine if the pulpit possesses any real substance behind it. However, there are also other reasons for a "powerless pulpit."

I have witnessed people who delivered the proper record or message, but there was no flame, life, or power to it. You can have the message, but, if you do not have the attitude to reinforce such a record, it will mean nothing to those who hear it.

What kind of attitude must those in the Christian pulpits have towards their place or position behind the pulpit? The Apostle Paul gives us insight into the type of attitude that must be evident when sharing heaven's record. Those who are proclaiming the message must realize they are in a battle for souls that is raging between light and darkness. These individuals must not only recognize this battle, but they must know how to bring the distinction between that which is of darkness and that which belongs to the light.

In *Ephesians 6*, we as Christians are given an armor that enables us to stand in faith, withstand with assurance, and stand in confidence in the battle. However, we have also been given a sword. This sword is powerful.

Once the sword is properly being executed against the real enemy, it will put him on the run. In fact, the sword is also a surgical knife that will expose the inner disposition or spirit of man. It will cut with truth, break down with conviction, and divide with purifying fire as a means to cleanse and bring healing, spiritual wholeness, and maturity to believers.

The Apostle Paul identifies this sword as being the Word of God. Jesus said of His words in *John 6:63* that they have Spirit and life. In other words, the witness of the Spirit is confirmed by the Word of God as it becomes milk and meat to the soul, renewing the inner man of the believers.

When the Holy Spirit sets God's people apart, it is referred to as the work of sanctification. Sanctification points to cleansing for the purpose of preparing the vessel to be made fit for the Master's use. Preparation of this nature entails establishing a right environment as a means for us, as believers, to offer each of our bodies as consecrated, living sacrifices that will be brought into compliance to the good, acceptable, and perfect will of God.[1]

The Holy Spirit distinguishes the believer by the work of sanctification that takes place in the inner man, but believers are also cleansed or sanctified through the truth of the Word.[2] Such cleansing cannot occur unless there is obedience. Obedience leads to conduct that will clearly distinguish or set believers a part from the dictates of self and the influence of the world.

When you study the work of God's uncompromising truth, you will realize that it separates in order to bring spiritual liberty to the life of a person. His truth establishes the environment in which a person can find their life in Christ. Such a liberating environment also allows the person to properly receive and to move forward to discover their potential in the kingdom of God.

Jesus spoke of the separation that the sword of truth would bring in *Matthew 10:32-35*. As you study these Scriptures, you can begin to see how sharp the truth of God's Word is. In *Matthew 10:32,* Jesus was talking about men denying Him before others. Keep in mind Jesus is the essence of all truth. If a matter does not

---

[1] Romans 12:1-2; 1 Peter 1:2
[2] John 17:17

line up to who He is, express His likeness in attitude and conduct, and become an example of His righteousness, man will, in essence, be denying Him in some way. Such denial means that a person is denying any real association or agreement with the record of heaven and disowning any point of identification of the revelation that has been clearly brought forth in the Word of God. *Matthew 10:31* actually identifies one of the main reasons people disassociate themselves with Jesus—fear.

Man often fears being associated with truth that is considered narrow and unloving by the world. Jesus explained why man has such a negative, repulsive response to this sharp sword. He stated that the truth takes away the cloak that hides the sin of man. This cloak is in place because man's natural preference is to maintain the darkness of his evil deeds, rather than having his deeds brought to the light by truth and reproved.[3]

The truth of God's Word brings a contrast between light and dark. It will call man to decide between the darkness of death and the light of life. It will ultimately make man responsible for his ways. However, truth that has not been anointed and inspired by heaven will be void of its sharpness. In other words, it is incapable of making any inroads into the soul and spirit of man.

Powerless truth has only the capacity to impact the intellect of man in the ways of information, facts, and doctrine, but not to expose the state of man's spirit and soul. Even though such lifeless truth may be correct, if it lacks the power to become revelation. Such information will simply feed the conceit of man, making him indifferent to the reality of God and his responsibility towards Him.

God's truth can only become life or revelation when the Spirit of God is anointing it with the sharpness to penetrate the spirit of man with the reality of God and His ways. The Spirit will use the Word of truth to convict people of their sin (revealing their real

---

[3] John 3:19-21; 15:22

spiritual state), reprove them of righteousness (bringing contrast between light and darkness), and warn them of judgment to come (contenting and exhorting man to repent before it is too late).[4]

This brings us to man's emphasis. If man is emphasizing the intellect according to man's take on theology and doctrine, the Holy Spirit will have no platform on which to make the truth sharp with conviction, righteousness, or judgment. Without the light of conviction that brings contrast, the Spirit will be prevented from bringing individuals to the place of conviction, repentance, understanding, and revelation. However, if man is emphasizing the record established in heaven according to the authority of the throne, the Holy Spirit will confirm, empower, and reveal the truth of it to open hearts.

The next aspect of truth is that it will divide where there is no real spiritual agreement. Although Jesus is the Prince of Peace, His sword of truth will bring contrast in order to establish a point of agreement.

Most people prefer their personal reality to God's unchanging truth. These same people may use the same terminology, but the spirit or intent behind their words is different in meaning, causing them to be far from the truth. As long as you remain surface with these people, they are able to hold onto their reality in darkness. However, when the sharpness of truth begins to penetrate these people's perceptions, conflict will naturally arise. It is at this point that any unholy attachments between people are cut, ripped, and torn, bringing separation. As Jesus pointed out in *Matthew 10:35-36,* such separation often begins in the home.

It is on the home front that our level of love for our Lord is often tested. The main reason people give into fear is because their love for God is fickle, weak, fleshly, and immature in light of the devotion they may have towards earthly family members or friends. This is why the Apostle John made this statement in *1*

---

[4] John 16:7-11; Ephesians 5:11-15

John 4:18-19, "There is no fear in love, but perfect love casteth out fear, because fear hath torment, He that feareth is not made perfect in love. We love him, because he first love us."

Jesus also stated that if a person loves family members more than Him, they will not be worthy to be considered as one belonging to Him. It is at this point Jesus reminded His followers that they must deny self of such entanglements and pick up their cross to ensure total separation from the world. This separation allows people to follow Him, and, as they follow Him, they will gain their life in Him. He also later identified those who are His family members as those who do the will of the Father.[5]

The sword of truth is meant to cut away that which has not been sanctified, rip away that which defiles, and tear away that which belongs to the old ways to ensure separation from that which entails unholy agreements. Truth is meant to put us on the same page as God in the matter of attitudes toward sin and the world. A right attitude is needed to establish righteousness according to the life of Jesus and to produce godly conduct that brings a clear distinction from that which belongs to darkness.

Sadly, people mishandle the truth by adjusting it to their particular reality. Adjusting truth renders it ineffective. The Holy Spirit will have no acceptable premise to bring revelation, causing the Word to fall by the wayside to be trampled by unbelief. Hence enters the warning that those who mishandle truth according to unrighteous motives and emphases will find themselves subject to the wrath of God.[6]

Without the powerful challenge of the sword of truth, man will be left in his dull state of compromise, darkness, and defeat. Since the truth is the only means by which to set the captive free, such a person will never know the victory of truth that will bring them to the blessed liberty of knowing God. Therefore, Christian pulpits

---

[5] Matthew 10:37-39; 12:46-50
[6] Romans 1:18

that do not know how to use God's Word as the sword of truth will fail to do battle for the souls of men.

This brings us back to the fact that the pulpit is a place to do battle. The truth must cut the necessary swath through congregations in order to bring the contrast that will serve as a mirror to those who call themselves Christians. The real spiritual state of people must be exposed so that the enemies of their souls can be properly discerned, addressed, and defeated. People must be given a choice of what head they will individually come into subjection to (Adam or Christ), what master they will serve (sin or God), and what husband they will submit to (the Law or the risen Christ).[7]

This brings us to the territory that is the focus of this unseen battle. The battleground comes down to faith. Although we have already dealt with the matter of faith in this book, we must once again examine it in light of the powerless pulpit. Repetition of spiritual truths causes us to approach such subjects from different angles. However, that which is of the truth will be confirmed in greater ways.

Jude wanted to talk about salvation, but instead, he found himself contenting or wrestling for the faith that was first delivered to the saints. As already stated, there are many counterfeit faiths being presented to Christendom. However, there is only one true faith according to the Bible, and Jesus wondered if He would find it when He came back as the King of kings and Lord of lords.[8]

We must constantly remind ourselves that faith is a choice. We must choose to believe and appropriate the Word as being true and not debate, adjust, or reject it. The true faith described in the Word comes by hearing the Word of God. As believers, we are to walk in obedience to the Word of God by faith. Acceptable faith

---

[7] Romans 5-7
[8] Luke 18:8; Ephesians 4:5; Jude 3

will direct its sole confidence, hope, and expectation towards the one true God. Such faith is the only means to please God.

In the armor of God, faith is the shield that gives us the confidence to stand on the truth of God when encountering the enemy, to withstand with His truth when attacked, and, when all is said and done in the battle, to continue to stand steadfast because of the truth of God's Word. We also know that faith is eternal and that at the end of it is our salvation. The Apostle Paul made the statement at the end of his life that he had kept the faith. Due to the importance of possessing the true faith, we are once again reminded of the apostle's exhortation to examine ourselves to see whether we are established in this faith. This faith can only be identified by the very life of Christ being present in us. It is His life that serves as our only true identification with Him and our hope of eternal glory.[9]

When God's shepherds stand behind pulpits, they must understand that they are contending for the faith that was first delivered to the saints. The battle can only be fought and won when the truth of God's sword is being presented under the anointing, inspiration, and power of the Spirit.

It is the sharpness and power of truth that will liberate souls to pursue, possess, and maintain this faith through the course of their lives. However, the battle can prove to be extreme, intense, and overwhelming to the shepherds. Satan attempts to rob God's people of unfeigned faith, the world strives to replace faith with worldly methods, and man's religion adjusts faith according to humanistic philosophies, while the darkness of unbelief slowly dulls the mind of man towards the Spirit's overtures and hardens his heart towards the truth.

Since faith has been replaced by methods and philosophies, the record of heaven is no longer emphasized in many of the

---

[9] Romans 10:17; 1 Corinthians 13:13; 2 Corinthians 13:5; Ephesians 6:16; Colossians 1:27; 2 Timothy 4:6-7; Hebrews 6:1; 11:1, 6; 1 Peter 1:9; 5:9

pulpits and teachings. Fleshly entertainment that excites the soul of man has taken the place of the move and work of the Holy Spirit. Meanwhile, the darkness of unbelief is invading the souls of men in the name of religion. This darkness is perceived as light, but, in reality, it is simply blinding these poor souls to the destruction that is awaiting them.

When the Apostle Paul exhorted people to examine to see if they were in the faith, he was establishing what each Christian must do to see if they are even in the same ballpark as God. When it comes to the matter of their salvation, people can believe they are saved and say they are saved, but, if they do not possess the true faith of the Bible, they remain lost.

What about you? When was the last time you actually examine yourself to see if you are on the same page as God when it comes to your faith?

14

PLACE OF AUTHORITY

We have been considering the reasons for the "powerless pulpit." We have looked at the record of heaven not being proclaimed or established through teaching. We know that, without the anointing of the Spirit, any such presentation will be lifeless, and, if the Word of truth is not sharpened by the Spirit, it will not impact anyone. When we combine these three elements together, we will be able to pinpoint one major reason for the pulpit being powerless. There is no authority present. Without authority, a preacher or teacher will not have the power to reinforce what is true.

How does one obtain authority? Authority can only be given by those who possess it. When you study Scripture, you realize there is only one who holds all authority, and that is God.

God clearly stipulates where authority has been given in the home, church, and His kingdom. Therefore, we can only reason that a pulpit that proves to be powerless does not have God's confirmation or approval. Without God's confirmation, a preacher or shepherd's word will not possess any real credibility. Granted, these religious leaders' words may sound entertaining and great and have the means to inspire the sentiment of the soul of man to respond, but they will never penetrate the spirit of man. It is in the spirit that man will know a matter is from God.

Authority has to do with rights that warrant a person's positions and claims with the intent to influence people concerning a matter. God must ordain a matter before it can be given credence. Once He ordains a matter, then He must ordain the person who will be entrusted to testify, proclaim, or present it to others. Such ordination signifies that God's authority is behind it, thereby giving the person who is ordained the right to influence people to weigh a matter out to ensure it has been properly sanctioned.

The Bereans are a good example of those who weighed out the preaching of Paul as to whether his message was truly sanctioned by God.[1] Once the authority of Paul's words was confirmed as being ordained by God, these people could readily receive his preaching, teachings, and instructions as truth.

This brings us back to what will warrant or sanction preaching or teaching from God's servants? As someone who has wrestled with this matter in the past, I have discovered some simple truths. Although, sometimes authority is interchanged with the word "power," there is a difference between these two words. Authority gives us the right to carry out a matter, while power enables us to carry it out. Without proper authority, power can prove to be abusive. After all, authority defines the purpose and direction of power that has been bestowed, while power will confirm the authority of the message that is presented.

When you listen to people, they mostly desire power as a means to exalt themselves and validate their claims. But, without proper authority, power has no real eternal purpose to it. If authority is clearly established in my life, power will naturally follow.

Sadly, I have watched people who held places of authority fail to be established in their positions. These people tried to exert power in their positions as a means to bring people into line with their agendas, but such self-serving methods do not possess the

---

[1] Acts 17:10-12

credibility to properly influence people. These particular individuals did not realize that sanctioned authority must be present to bring order to the situation.

There are four reasons why people mishandle authority. The first one is inexperience. Inexperienced people tend to become prideful when they are entrusted with authority they have not been prepared to walk in, rather than seeing it as a grave responsibility. This is why the Bible tells us not to place novices in leadership positions in *1 Timothy 3:6*.

Another way authority is mishandled is through abusing one's position. People who abuse authority have never learned how to recognize or respect it in other people's lives. They see authority as their personal platform to exert their agendas, selfishness, and demands on others.

The third way people mishandle authority is through neglect. They do not recognize the responsibility established by their position. As a result, they become indifferent to their responsibility and drop the ball in terms of ensuring respect, discipline, and order.

Without discipline in the environment, chaos will prevail, preventing people from being prepared to properly receive. A chaotic environment will create disrespect towards all authority. We can see this in the case of many homes. Children call the shots, rather than the parents who were given the authority by God to influence their children by training them in the ways of righteousness.

Righteousness expresses itself by recognizing and honoring that which possesses authority. Since the ways of righteousness are missing in these homes, there is chaos. The children struggle with their place in the family as they lack any sense of real security. Insecurity turns into anger as these children begin to express their frustration by becoming disobedient and disrespectful towards their parent's authority. Eventually, this disrespect will take root and create lawlessness in the children. Lawlessness refuses to respect any authority or boundaries.

The fourth way people mishandle authority is by overstepping it. These are the people who add their own twists or standards to what they have been entrusted with. When people overstep their boundaries, it often causes confusion and division in a matter.

When it comes to our authority as Christians, we must understand where it comes from and how it is to be properly established in our lives. We know our power comes from the Holy Spirit. However, this power is to be clearly tested, disciplined, and executed according to the authority we possess. Keep in mind that authority comes from those who have the right to sanction or ordain a matter. As Christians, our authority comes from Jesus. The reason I say this is because of what Jesus said in *John 17:18, "As thou hast sent me into the world, even so have I also sent them into the world."* Since Jesus sent us forth, our authority comes from Him.

Clearly, Jesus has a reason to send us forth into the world. But, what has He entrusted to us? We already know that we have been entrusted with the record of heaven. However, we must consider how this record will establish us in our authority.

There are a couple of ways we, as Christians, become established in this authority. The first aspect of authority that must be present to verify our credibility is agreement. There is no way a person of authority can entrust you or me with a matter unless there is agreement. Jesus brought this out in *John 17:21, "That they all may be one, as thou, Father art in me, and I in thee, that they also may be one in us; that the world may believe that thou hast sent me."*

At the very core of the record of heaven is the Person and work of Jesus. Who is the person of Jesus? We have already addressed this issue, but we must recognize that it is hard for people to realize that the great debate at the heart of heaven's record is Jesus' identity. As pointed out, some say that Jesus is just a "good" man, a "great" prophet, a high-ranking angel, or one of the way-showers of this present age. Some claim His conscience is what prevails in the world and that possessing it causes them to become deified. However, such beliefs are contrary to the record of heaven.

Obviously, Jesus can be anyone or anybody. He can be given certain entitlements, but, if He is not revealed to the spirit or heart of man by heaven, man will erect a lifeless or conceptual Jesus. This Jesus may run parallel with the Bible, or he may even line up to the Bible's revelation, but such a Jesus will lack authority.

There is only one real Jesus. He can only be known when He is unveiled by heaven to our spirits. The Jesus of the Bible is not a theory, image, or fantasy. He is a living Person. In fact, the record of heaven declares that Jesus is fully God and fully man. He is God who came in the flesh to walk in the midst of man, ultimately dying on the cross for the sins of man.

Once again, we are reminded that the Apostle Paul described Jesus' coming in the flesh as being the mystery of godliness that was clearly revealed to man.[2] The mystery of godliness identifies the reality of God (manifested in the flesh), His witness (justified and upheld in the Spirit), His confirmation (seen of the angels), proclaimed as Lord and Savior (preached unto the Gentiles), received as truth (believed on in the world), and ensured His Person and work (received up into glory).

The Apostle John clearly identified Jesus possessing the glory of God from heaven. In His prayer just before Calvary, Jesus made reference to His glory as God in *John 17:5, "And now, O Father, glorify thou me with thine own self with the glory which I had with thee before the world was."*

In light of this record, can people believe another Jesus and be saved, or are they actually neglecting such a great salvation?

---

[2] 1 Timothy 3:16

Keep in mind, Jesus is the essence of truth. If a person does not believe the record concerning Jesus, they will not possess the light of God. In fact, such individuals are calling God a liar because they will not receive the truth, regardless of the clear record that has been presented in His Word, confirmed by His Spirit, and established by the covenant wrought by Jesus' blood.[3]

One of the reasons pulpits remain powerless is because the people who stand behind them have not believed the record concerning Jesus. The Father draws people to the Son, Jesus invites people to come to Him, and the Holy Spirit leads a person into all truth concerning Him.[4] Since these people do not believe that Jesus is who the Bible ascribes Him to be, they have no agreement with heaven; therefore, they have no authority.

The Apostle Paul made this statement about those who are being tossed to and fro by every wind of doctrine: "*Till we all come in the unity of the faith, and of the knowledge of the Son of God, unto a perfect man, unto the measure of the stature of the fullness of Christ*" *(Ephesians 4:13).*

Without agreement with heaven, a person can be assured that Jesus will never send them forth to carry out a mission. Such a person would not have the credibility to back up their claims.

This brings us to the second point about authority. Without authority, one does not have the power to make an eternal impact. In *Matthew 28:18b-20,* Jesus gave this commission to His disciples,

> *All power is given unto me in heaven and in earth. Go ye, therefore, and teach all nations, baptizing them in the name of the Father, and of the Son, and of the Holy Ghost, Teaching them to observe all things whatsoever I have commanded you; and, lo, I am with you always, even unto the end of the world. Amen.*

---

[3] Romans 3:1-4; Hebrews 2:3
[4] John 6:44; 7:37-38; 14:26; 16:13-14

Keep in mind that authority defines our responsibility, while power enables us to carry out our commission.

Jesus clearly stipulated why He was sending us out in the world. Our commission is two-fold in these Scriptures. We are to teach all nations to observe all things concerning the matters of heaven. Teaching points to instructing people how to effectively live the Christian life. Observing all things involves obeying what has clearly been established as our godly responsibility. Observation of His commandments will ensure us that He will be with us, even to the end of the age.

The second part of this commission is to baptize people in the name or according to the character of the Father, of the Son, and of the Holy Ghost. Once again, we have the three witnesses of heaven that remind us of the record that was set forth. Water baptism points to total identification with Jesus in His life and work. Such identification will have no meaning if a person fails to live the life that is associated with it.

Likewise, our heavenly authority has no meaning or purpose if we do not fulfill our commission. Authority will be present in obedience, but missing in disobedience. Sadly, there are those who stand behind Christian pulpits, preaching another Jesus, operating according to a different spirit, and adhering to another gospel. These people's words will not possess any power, their works will be considered reprobate, and they will stand condemned by the Judge of heaven.

Do you sense authority coming from the pulpit of your fellowship? If not, it could be because your pastor has never really been ordained by heaven to be in his position, or, perhaps, the words he speaks do not have power behind them because he is not really fulfilling his commission according to his high calling. Only you can discern if the particular pulpit at your church building possesses the authority to impact the eternal destination of the souls of people.

15

VISION

When we consider the possible reasons that some of our pulpits in America and throughout the world are "powerless," we must examine the concept of vision. Vision has to do with the vantage point from which we consider a matter. The wisest man in the Old Testament stated that people who did not possess vision would perish.[1]

It must be noted that people examine all things from what they consider to be their particular vantage point. Some believe their intellectual abilities are a vantage point. Others perceive their sentimental insights, particularly those that involve religion and its practices, as vantage points. Some consider their vantage point in light of the ability to logic out a matter, while there are those who see their superior position because of the facts they possess.

When we consider these vantage points, we must recognize that our frame of reference or our worldview is usually what serves as our vantage point. However, such a perspective has been greatly influenced by the world's philosophies. Whenever the things of the flesh or the world are involved when it comes to our point of consideration, we must acknowledge that we are earthbound. In fact, our perceptions taint what we do perceive because we cannot see beyond self or above the influences or activities of the world.

---

[1] Proverbs 29:18

The Apostle Paul spoke of blindness that plagues man who relies on the vantage point of the world. He explained in *2 Corinthians 4:3-6* that the god of this present age or world has actually blinded such people towards the light of the true Gospel, ensuring their spiritual destruction.

Jesus also in *Matthew 6:22-23* explained the delusion that is established by this false light or vantage point when He declared that, even though such understanding is darkness, it will seem as if it is light to the spiritually blind. Such a darkness of delusion can prove great since it is blinding these people to the destructive path they are on.

"Powerless pulpits" lack spiritual vision. Granted, some pastors have a vision for church growth, bringing in more money, and establishing greater outreaches, but such vision reveals that the pastor is earthbound. When we consider what the Word of God states, we must recognize that God did not send His disciples out to build greater church buildings, establish greater ministries, develop better methods to gain financial support, or devise noteworthy plans to reach many people. Jesus' instructions to the disciples were clear: preach the Gospel and teach people to observe or obey His commandments.

Since our Lord's instructions are clear, why is it that some Church leaders are emphasizing the pursuits of the world? Granted, such pursuits may sound noble and acceptable, but such emphasizes or pursuits will not bring salvation to any one. Such promotion is nothing more than advocating a social gospel that may help, impress, and attract people, but salvation will still be missing from the agenda.

A man stated his concern for the particular church he was affiliated with. He shared how he remembered when they preached the Gospel and the members were alive with inspiration. However, he recently noticed that nothing was really happening. As a church body, they appeared to be in a time warp in which they could not move backward to clearly discern their condition or forward in spiritual growth.

Since I had no first-hand knowledge of the church, my guess was that the leadership may have started off right, but it got off track. I then explained that all a church body has to do to get off track is to change its emphasis from what Christ has ordained and commissioned His Church to do, to something that is earthbound and will ultimately prove lifeless and uninspired.

There was a pastor of a big church who admitted to me that he had created a monster that he barely could keep ahead of. In fact, I wondered how much of his time he had to put in trying to finance the monstrosity that he had developed in his attempts to look like a successful pastor of a growing church. I observed him preaching about causes, while tacking a weak gospel on the end of his message to justify his preaching. What I did not see was people truly coming to salvation.

As we consider the pursuit and emphasis of some Christian Churches, it is becoming more apparent that the pastors, along with some who are in their congregations, have lost their way. The main reason people do not know where they are going is because they have lost sight of where they started from. In summation, they have lost their focus. They have become entangled in the terrain of the world and loaded down by the endless demands of a self-serving, religious lifestyle that leaves them empty and full of despair.

The Apostle Paul explained what the Christian's vantage point should be in *Ephesians 2:6, "And hath raised us up together, and made us sit together in heavenly places in Christ Jesus."* Positionally, we have been placed in high places in Jesus. For Christians, this position means that their vantage point is a heavenly one and not earthbound by worldly aspirations that have no sense of the spiritual or eternal perspective. When we compare the heavenly vantage point to the earthbound one, the contrast is quite clear.

Those who have an earthbound vantage point have no vision past this present world. Without a heavenly vision, there is no direction, inspiration, or real purpose. Without spiritual vision, man is not only blind to the paths and traps of destruction and death, but he is assured of losing his way and possibly his very soul.

In his book *God's Goal: Christ as All in All,* Manfred Haller stated that the main problem with the Church at Ephesus, mentioned in *Revelation 2:1-7,* is that the people had lost their vantage point of being seated in heavenly places with Christ. Even though they were technically on, they had lost their sense of true identification, direction, and purpose. Clearly, it was not just a matter of doing "good" works and standing for truth, it was a matter of viewing all things from the heavenly perspective. It is the heavenly perspective that keeps the influences and demands of this present age in the right order.

Obviously, there are pastors who have fallen into the traps of the world. They are viewing matters from the premise of the world's idea of success and significance. As a result, their pulpits have been rendered powerless by worldly compromises, emphases, and agreements.

Obviously, our pulpits must be taken back. For this to happen, pastors, teachers, and leaders need to align their vision to that which is ordained by God. This ordination has been clearly exalted in the heavenlies and possesses the eternal. It is from this vantage point that pastors and congregations can experience the fire and power of heaven.

In order to possess a heavenly perspective, God's people must come to terms with what it means to possess such a vantage point. We were given this prophesy concerning the last days in *Acts 2:17-18,*

And it shall come to pass in the last days, saith God, I will pour out of my Spirit upon all flesh; and your sons and your daughters shall prophesy, and your young men shall see visions, and your old men shall dream dreams; And on my servants and on my handmaidens I will pour out in those days of my Spirit, and they shall prophesy.

It is important to note that, in the last days, God will pour out His Spirit upon all flesh. On Pentecost, the beginning of the end days started for this present age. Granted in light of earthly time, for the Church, this has been a long stretch of two thousand years as far as the last days. But, the most important aspect about the age of the Church will be the presence and power of the Spirit. He will not only reside in believers, but He will be poured out on believers to empower them to walk out their Christian lives, boldly carry out their commission, and inspire the direction of their vision. Obviously, the vision that every believer must possess will be marked by the presence of eternity. It will not be based on what we know or understand as Christians; rather, it will be inspired by the Holy Ghost.

The Holy Spirit is the one who gives revelations to believers. A revelation is the unveiling of a spiritual truth or matter about our Lord to bring inspiration, instruction, wisdom, and spiritual growth to Christians. Such unveiling is God's way of speaking His reality into the hearts of His people. However, this spiritual reality will not only leave people with a greater understanding of Scripture, but also a greater sense and knowledge of the character and ways of God.

In the youthful days of the prophet Samuel, it says that the word of the Lord was rare, and that there was no open or frequent vision in those days. The people of Israel had the Law, but an ongoing revelation or unveiling of God's heart and truths were missing due to the sin of the priesthood. However, this environment changed when Samuel was a man. It is said that

Samuel grew and the Lord was with him. But, one of the reasons the Lord was with Samuel is that he did not let the words he proclaimed as both man and prophet fall to the ground.[2] He held them tight and maintained their integrity.

Remember, when we consider matters through the glasses of the flesh and the world, all we see will be darkened, tainted, or perverted. However, when we possess the heavenly vantage point, we are considering everything through the Person of Jesus Christ, who is *all truth*. We have been seated in high places *in* Christ who will serve as the frame or glasses through which we examine all matters.

This brings us to the work of the Spirit. He is the one who leads us into all truth about Jesus. He leads us to an understanding of Christ in order to unveil Him to us in a greater measure. Each unveiling brings us to a greater knowledge of Jesus that will even more so transform how we look at life. It is through our enlarged perspective that we will be lifted up in greater heights in His glory.

The Bible clearly brings out and confirms the truth about revelation. Such heavenly vision is what the Lord's people must pursue, possess, and live in accordance to. Each vision simply enlarges the person's understanding of God. There are four examples we are going to consider.

The first example is Moses. Moses ascended into the presence of God on Mount Sinai. He was there for forty days and nights and received the Law. However, his request after Mount Sinai revealed the type of focus that was inspired and defined by his experience in the presence of God. Heed what he asked of God in *Exodus 33:18, "And he said, I beseech thee, show me thy glory."* Moses was not seeking personal greatness, nor would he settle for simply experiencing God's presence. His heart was panting after an even greater revelation of Him that could only be unveiled in the light of His unending glory.

---

[2] 1 Samuel 3:1, 17-18

The prophet Isaiah's vision revolutionized his life.[3] He saw the Lord sitting upon a throne, high and lifted up, as his train filled the temple. We cannot begin to comprehend the indelible impact that this vision had on Isaiah. He sensed his unworthiness in light of the Lord's holiness. He cried out to be purged, and, once he stood purged, he was ready to offer his services, even in light of the fact that people would not hear him in their state of spiritual dullness.

Clearly, revelation has the ability to revolutionize God's people. However, the vision is of God's greatness or majesty. Such visions will humble and cause His true servants to avail themselves to His mission.

A vision that beholds the majesty of the Son of God will transform and enlarge one's spiritual ability to see into the depths of God's character. It will also allow His saints to witness incredible aspects of the heights and brightness of His glory, even in spite of the present darkness of the age that may surround them.

The Apostle Paul actually loss his physical eyesight when he encountered the true light of the world.[4] The reality of our vision is that the physical eyes cannot behold the glory of God without being blinded by it. Such glory will reveal the darkness of one's soul, as it envelops them with the sense of total depravity and hopelessness. The example that Paul leaves us with is that the only way we will not be blinded by the heavenly light is to allow God to open the spiritual eyes of our hearts so we can truly behold the Son of God.

The Apostle Paul explained that there is a veil or covering over our spiritual eyes that prevent us from seeing the Lord in the spirit. He stated that only the Lord can take away the veil so we can see Him in His glory. As we come into the place of witnessing His glory

---

[3] Isaiah 6
[4] Acts 9

and partaking of His very life, we will actually begin to take on His glory and reflect it to the world.[5]

The Apostle John also received an unveiling of Christ in *Revelation 1.* In fact, the whole theme of the book is Christ being unveiled as God, and coming back as victorious King and righteous Judge. Granted, many perceive Jesus as Savior and Lord, but, when Jesus comes back to claim the throne of David, He will come as the great Alpha and the never-ending Omega to execute judgment on the rebellious world. His entrance is going to cause those who have opposed Him to beg the rocks to fall on them as a means to hide them from His face that will reveal the extent of His great wrath that is ready to be poured out.[6]

Amazingly, John's reaction to the new revelation of the Christ was unexpected, but it sends a clear message to each of us. This apostle had been part of the inner group who witnessed miracles and the parting of Christ's humanity to reveal His glory as deity on the Mount of Transfiguration. He had laid his head on Jesus' chest the night He was betrayed. Jesus had entrusted the care of His mother, Mary, to him. He had been tempered by persecution, refined by the fires of adversity, and firmly established on the immovable Rock of Jesus. However, when Jesus was unveiled to him in Revelation, he fell at Jesus' feet as if dead. Jesus lifted him up and introduced Himself as the *"I am" that lived, was put to death, but now is alive evermore.* He is the one who now holds the keys of hell and death.[7]

As reminded by *Hebrews 2:14* in regard to the keys, *"Forasmuch, then, as the children are partakers of flesh and blood, he also himself likewise took part of the same, that through death he might destroy him that had the power of death, that is the devil."*

---

[5] 2 Corinthians 3:6-18
[6] Revelation 6:16-17
[7] Revelation 1:17-18

As we meditate on each of these examples, we, as believers, must realize that our vision must be the Son of God. As each of us considers these men, we can see that they were not seeking greater ministry, acknowledgment, methods, or miracles; rather, they were seeking to behold their Lord in greater measure.

If God people's vision was heavenward, their vantage point would be from and through Jesus. From this vantage point, they would and will be able to view the finished work of redemption, the ongoing ministry of Jesus as the High Priest, and the reality of God's heart toward the loss world. Such a perception will allow them to experience the leading of the Spirit according to God's eternal plan.

Pulpits that are aflame with the presence and power of the Spirit are pulpits where the pastor, leader, or teacher has beheld the Son of God on a continual basis. They have established and disciplined this heavenly focus by daily aligning their vision heavenward towards the One who sits on the right hand of God.

As they align their vision upward, they set their affections on Jesus, knowing that they are dead in Him, to their self-lives and the influences of the world. As these people set their hearts towards Jesus, their faith in Him becomes steadfast as they truly connect to the throne, heart, and purpose of God. In light of their heavenly connection, they also know that, because of their new lives in Jesus, they are actually hid in Him, and, when He appears, they are confident that they will also appear with Him in glory.[8]

How many leaders have you met that possess a heavenly focus? If you have met such a person, you might have taken note of their eyes. There is something about their eyes that can draw you to them, while causing you to feel unnerved and exposed. It is as though the penetrating ability of these individuals' eyes is capable of undoing a person. The transparency of their eyes reveals a light that is not of the present world; therefore, they are

---

[8] Colossians 3:1-4

capable of penetrating its thick darkness. The intensity of their eyes is like a fire that burns through the coverings, masks, and cloaks to reveal the heart of a matter. Ultimately, the eyes of these people will reveal that they have seen into heaven itself.

In summation, these people have seen the essence of beauty, heard unspeakable words that cannot be comprehended by fleshly ears, and witnessed the miraculous, for they have beheld the mystery of godliness as described by *Isaiah 9:6*.

They have seen the one who is too wonderful to comprehend. They have heard His wisdom as the ultimate Counselor. They have experienced His power as The Mighty God. They have been touched by His love as The Everlasting Father. They have smelled and partaken of the sweetness of His peace as the Prince of Peace. They have indeed beheld the Son of God in His glory.

What about you? Have you recently beheld the Son of God? Is He your focus, or is your vision limited by that which has no connection to the depths or heights of the eternal and the heavenly?

Part IV

COMING BACK
TO CENTER

16

ARISE SLEEPING CHURCH

What does it mean for the Church of Jesus to come back to the center of what is truly inspired by the Spirit and established by the truth? We know that the real Church is local, national, and universal. The first thing we must recognize is not everyone who calls themselves Christian is part of Jesus' Body. Not every denomination or belief that wears the handle of being Christian represents or advocates the interests of the kingdom of heaven. The images that are being presented by some of the visible Church may have another spirit behind their religious cloaks or robes. The gospel that is being presented in some camps may be watered-down with compromise, perverted with worldliness, or tainted with poisonous heresy.

When it comes to the universal Church, it is hard to say how much of it, if any, has strayed from the center. Due to some of the influences and inroads worldly Christianity has made into certain mission fields, I realize that there are those who belong to the universal Church who have adopted worldly, greedy, unscriptural attitudes of the western Church. Much of the Church is being persecuted in different places throughout the world.

The stories of Christians being persecuted for the sake of Christ are incredible, yet these people know they only have one life to offer, and they are willing to offer their bodies as living sacrifices to their precious Lord, as well as in light of the living testimony He has established in the hearts of many.

The environment of the local churches around the world, along with their challenges, will vary. This is why studying the epistles and the seven churches in *Revelation 2-3* shows how each church had a different struggle keeping to the center of Spirit and truth. Some local churches seemed more successful than other bodies. The main factors that caused the difference were probably being determined by the quality of leadership and environment.

For example, in Romans, Paul dealt with the realities of the simple Gospel, which included sin, faith, justification, reconciliation, identification, and the work of the Spirit. The first letter to the Corinthians dealt with carnality, discipline, and the Oral Law of the Jews, while the second letter addressed such subjects as consolation, repentance, ministry, and benevolence. Galatians confronted the place the Law was to have in the Christian's life. Ephesians addressed our inheritance as believers, Philippians dealt with what constituted godly attitude, Colossians contended with the matter of Christ's deity and pre-eminence, and Thessalonians spoke of the Christian's assurance and blessed hope.

The question is what kind of exhortation needs to be given to the Church in America? Granted, there are many different bodies, but the issue comes down to the prevailing environment that can be clearly discerned on a national level. Is there such an environment present? I believe there is.

Due to the compromise with the world, some of the Church is basically asleep. Like the idolatrous people of Israel, this unholy agreement with the world has caused the hearts of some in the Church to become gross, their ears dull of hearing, and their eyes closed to the reality around them. The problem is that they have no intention of being converted to that which would oppose their particular reality in order to truly be healed by God's truth.

This brings us to the challenge that is confronting the American Church. The Apostle Paul made this statement, *"That he might present it to himself a glorious church, not having spot, or wrinkle, and any such thing; but that it should be holy and without blemish" (Ephesians 5:27).* Jesus is coming for a Church that is chaste, not one that reveals inconsistencies due to moral deviations, unholy alliances, and unscriptural variations in its foundation and conduct.

Sadly, much of the Church in America has become another subculture in the midst of many multi-cultures. The problem is that it is simply going with the waves of tolerance that have been rolling through America.

However, Christianity was never meant to become a subculture with its own lingo and ethnic practices. Christianity is about living the life of Jesus in the midst of the world. It is the distinction of His life that will identify and distinguish the Christian in the world. After all, as believers, our commission is not to get others to agree or share in the subculture of Christianity; it is to offer the life-giving message of Jesus so that people can become the children of God. As children of God, these people will not only be identified with an eternal inheritance that is not of this present world, but they also will become citizens of a heavenly kingdom that will distinguish them as priests and kings.

With this in mind, the Church in America must come to terms with what it will take to ensure that it possesses such a chaste environment. After all, how much of the Church is finding itself riding the high wave of living a worldly lifestyle that enjoys and partakes of temporary benefits, while trying to maintain an active testimony of separation and distinction from such influences?

The truth is that we are living in precarious times. The wave that America has been enjoying is beginning to slam against the shoreline of reality. It is about to reap the whirlwind of judgment due to its idolatry and its overindulgence in selfishness, rebellion, immorality, and hatred towards God.

Although many live in denial about this nation's condition, as well as deny the Scriptures that address the last days, if Americans remain unrepentant, this great nation will inevitably become shipwrecked as it hits the rocks of destruction. Its demise will expose the attitude many have developed towards it for the last four decades. Like Jerusalem during God's judgment on it, America will become a byword that once was marked by greatness, but, because the values that were written into her very fiber have been compromised, mocked, and discarded by the unchecked agendas of the wicked, it could very well end up lying in utter ruin. In summation, some of the people of America are literally pulling this nation down around our ears.

What will happen to the visible Church since aspects of it are part of this wave of destruction? It is important to point out that many people in America are asleep to the impending destruction. They are caught up with fantasies and notions that are blinding them to the collision course this nation is on. Sadly, much of the Church that has been riding this wave is asleep as well.

Therefore, the first course of action is that the sleeping members of the Church must awake from their spiritual dullness to properly face the course this nation is on. Once they face it, they must take responsibility for not only their spiritual condition, but the condition of this nation. By compromising with the world, much of the visible Church has failed to bring a viable contrast between light and dark. Without distinction from the world, it does not possess the authority it needs to warn and exhort others.

It must be noted that Christians are not only called to be preachers and teachers, but watchmen. They are not only to guard their inward condition, their homes, and their churches against invading enemies, but they are to watch the condition of the times that they are living in. After all, watchmen are to warn others of what is coming on the horizon. However, when Christians are sleeping instead of watching, they will not be ready to hear the warnings or prepared to properly respond.

It is important at this time to point out that the destruction that has been prophesized concerning the end of the last days will not be expected by most people. Many will be asleep, snuggled under the covering of a false peace. The destruction that is coming will come as a thief, ready to rob, kill, and destroy.[1]

This destruction will not sneak through the door, it will suddenly knock it down. This is why the Apostle Paul reminded Christians in *1 Thessalonians 5:5-9* that they are children of the light. As a result, they must not sleep as others who refuse to face the reality of the times; rather, they must be watching and sober-minded.

He goes on to say that those who are asleep are as if they are drunk in the night. Therefore, as alert Christians, we must put on the breastplate of faith and love, as well as the helmet that serves as the hope of salvation to maintain our spiritual edge as watchmen. As reliable watchmen, we will be guarding with the sword of truth against the invasion of darkness, knowing we will ultimately be spared from God's wrath to come.

Clearly, those of the Church must awake before it is too late to not only sound the warning, but to be prepared to act. The Apostle Paul's instructions were clear about Christians who are drunk with sleep. He commanded them to awake and arise from the state of death, enabling Christ to give them the light to see what is going on.[2]

The apostle went on to command these sleepy individuals to awake to righteousness and cease from sinning. Keep in mind that the drunken state of slumber is the result of many of these individuals partaking of the world to the point they are intoxicated by it. In their state, the darkness of unbelief has overtaken them

---

[1] John 10:10; 1 Thessalonians 5:2-4
[2] Ephesians 5:14

because they not only have become unfruitful and barren in their knowledge of Jesus, but they are also suffering from a famine of the Word of God. They have failed to fill their lives up with the things of God by following after righteousness that establishes a person on the Rock, as well as faith that is directed towards God, charity that is expressed in benevolent actions, and the peace that comes only from Christ.[3]

In *Romans 13:11-14* the Apostle Paul exhorted believers to awake, knowing the time. Clearly, for us in this age, time is short, and the reality of the fullness of salvation is nearer than when each of us first believed. The night that has engulfed many in this present age has been far spent; therefore, it is time to cast off the works of darkness that have been at work in our lives and put on the armor of light.

To put on the armor of light simply means to put on the Lord Jesus with the intent of walking in integrity according to all that is upright before Him. If we put on the life of Jesus, we will not make provision for the flesh, thereby, putting off its lust with its rebellion, drunken ways, immoral practices, covetous pursuits, contrary attitudes, and jealous demands.

The challenge is clear. As the Church, we must awake from beneath the dark cover of deception, repent of our hardened hearts of idolatry, and ask the Lord to take the veil of compromise from our eyes and the plugs of indifference from our ears. We must allow the heavy hand of the Potter to soften our hearts with humility to ensure that we are able to respond to His conviction. We must desire Him to heal our eyes with the salve of truth so they can clearly see the destruction that is coming on the horizon and clean out our ears in order to hear what the Spirit is saying so that we can respond to the call of God.

At this time in history, God is shaking America as never before. The markets are in the flux of uncertainty and chaos, as the great

---

[3] Amos 8:11; 1 Corinthians 15:34; 2 Timothy 2:22; 2 Peter 1:8-9

idol of wealth is beginning to be broken up in various pieces, and its remaining residues taken out into the ocean of foolishness by the great wave of judgment. The banks are beginning to hoard money, creating an environment of financial depression, smaller businesses are now becoming casualties to greed, and the American lifestyle is dissipating as despair is taking hold of many families.

Due to the elections of 2008, the government is now purporting socialistic practices that are anti-God, anti-Israel, and contrary to the Constitution of this nation. In these wicked people's quick attempt to socialize all institutions to bring them under the government as a means to usher people into communistic control and oppression, America will cease to exist, along with its government. What is sad is these leaders are foolishly fouling their own nest, as the powers of the world are considering how to divide this country which is clearly split in its philosophies.

The question is where is the Church of America? How much of the Church is being shipwrecked by the shaking that is taking place because it has been asleep? Sadly, being shipwrecked at the point of faith is not the same as being cleansed. It simply shows that faith has not been towards God, and such revelation will leave those who feel the sharpness of the rocks, reeling in utter despair. Once again, faith is not refined by the rocks of judgment, but by the fiery ovens of adversities.[4]

Remember, the Church will be presented to Jesus in a chaste state. No doubt, God is beginning the process. As stated, judgment does not refine, it simply reveals the quality of something in order to separate it for the purpose to purify it or to deliver it to wrath. Judgment is a dividing point, a crossroad where a decision will be required by the person who is facing the devastation. Will the person choose to trust God, humble self to seek His face, or will they allow the waves of judgment to take

---

[4] 1 Timothy 1:19; 1 Peter 1:5-9

what is left of their shambled lives in Christ out into the ocean of wrath and destruction?

Those who belong to the true Church of Jesus must choose to trust Him, regardless of what is going on. Those who experience any type of shipwreck of their lives in Christ must realize it is the result of them failing to truly hide in the ark of Christ. They have allowed the currents of the world to move them towards this point, rather than giving way to the powerful air currents of the Holy Spirit.

The Church must be purified by the washing of the Word or the fire of the Holy Spirit. If it is not purified by God's tools, He will use adversities such as persecution, losses, and failure to rid His people of the various contaminates of self, the world, and works of darkness.

However, as His people, we must be part of the cleansing that must take place in our lives to ensure a chaste environment in our homes and for the Church. *James 4:6-10* talks about what it means to be cleansed. Those who need to be purified must first come to a state of humility. From this premise, they can actually submit themselves before God. Such submission will allow them to actually resist the devil, causing him to flee.

Since the interference of darkness is no longer present, God's people are able to repent. Repentance is a turning away from the old dark ways in order to turn and face the Lord and draw near to Him. As *James 4:6-10* tells us, this will allow the Lord to draw near to the repentant, humble soul with the intent to lift them up out of the mire of their pit. It is within His presence that people's hands can be cleansed from touching that which is unclean, and hearts can be purified from divided loyalties. As His people become afflicted in their spirits because of what their treacherous actions have cost God, their souls will become mournful as their sins are revealed. From this premise, they will begin to be broken at the point of their pride, as they feel the depth of heaviness tighten its vice-grip on their feeble frames of humanity.

Brokenness of spirit towards sin is a much-needed sacrifice before God that would produce the environment of healing, reconciliation, and restoration. It is able to ensure the revival of the spirit, the transformation of the soul, and the reformation of one's outer conduct.

How many of those who claim to be part of Jesus' Church would be willing to go through such a process to gain His life and ensure a right inward environment? The problem is that many of these individuals do not see how far from the center they are. They perceive themselves good enough in regard to their Christian life. They do not realize that their perceptions about religious matters are serving as their personal center; rather than God, whose thoughts and ways are far above man's.

This brings us to the need of contrast. Without the mirror of truth, man will never see how far from the center he is. To sense his spiritual plight, he must have a revelation of how the Christian life will express itself. After all, it must be an expression of Jesus and not of man's best attempts or the world's best presentation. There is no substitution to this life.

In the next chapter, I am going to rise up the mirror of the real purpose and working of the Church. I am then going to follow it up in the next chapter with how the Body of Christ has been divided as a means to conquer it. Ultimately, in the final chapter, I will be ending with the promise that has been given to those who are truly members of the Body of Christ.

Meanwhile, consider if you are riding the wave of the world. Perhaps you have already hit the rocks of the shoreline of reality, and your faith has been left shipwrecked as you are struggling with what to do next. Maybe you are aware that something is not quite right about your spiritual life and understanding. The answer can be found in humility before God, submission to His Spirit, and obedience to His Word.

17

UNVEILING THE MYSTERY

We have considered the different aspects of the challenge confronting the Church. The members of this body need a spiritual vision or revelation that will awake them from any spiritual slumber as a means to encourage them to finish the course set before them.

Vision or focus is vital because it allows the person to keep their eyes on the goal. As we consider the different paths that some of the professing Church have taken, we must consider if many in this visible Church lack such vision when it comes to the function, purpose, and goal God established in regard to the Body of Jesus.

Obviously, before we can actually confront the problems ailing the professing Church, we must first establish God's perspective of it. Even though this book has brought glimpses of the purpose of the Body of Christ, it needs to be clearly established. In *Ephesians 5:22-33,* the Apostle Paul explained how marriage pointed to the type of relationship that Jesus wanted with His Church.

The mystery that was unveiled by Christ in regard to the Church is that He wanted to be one with this Body as He is one with the Father. Godly marriage was to unveil such a relationship of oneness to the world. We are given insight into this very fact in *John 17:23, "I in them, and thou in me, that they may be made perfect in one; and that the world may know that thou hast sent me, and has loved them, as thou has loved me."*

We know that the Church's commission is to preach the Gospel and disciple believers to be followers of Christ. However, its authority to do so comes from the Head, Jesus Christ. Its power is realized when that oneness or agreement with Jesus is present. Jesus confirmed this very fact when He stated that, where there are two or three in agreement, matters can be accomplished and brought forth through prayer.[1]

As we consider the oneness that should be present in marriage, we even become more aware of how such agreement is brought forth. Marriage points to a vow, a covenant, and walking as one in a way that will serve as a living testimony. A vow is where a person agrees to fulfill certain requirements in regard to his or her relationship with the other party. A vow in marriage points to the act of consecration in which the couple separates from all others in order to separate themselves to each other. Therefore, the couple's vow is one of faithfulness towards one another.

A covenant is perpetual or ongoing. It points to the responsibilities that those who enter this agreement must maintain in order to ensure the integrity of their relationship. In marriage, the woman must submit to that which is worthy, her Lord Jesus, to ensure the *intent* of the marriage, and man must love his wife as Christ loved the Church to ensure the *integrity* of this relationship.

In the past, covenants usually entailed the offering of sacrifices to show commitment to this agreement. These sacrifices sealed the agreement as being true. In the covenant of marriage, sacrifices are also required. Submission points to the voluntary sacrifice of consecration that had to be made with every offering made by the priest. Without the consecration or separation unto

---

[1] Matthew 18:19-20

God, sacrifices do not possess any real distinctions that are clearly marked by true devotion. These types of sacrifices emitted smoke or a fragrance that was pleasing to God. Although such sacrifices represented reasonable service, they also spoke of man's desire to please God and show due service and honor to Him.

As the voluntary sacrifice, the wife is able to submit to her husband in light of her devotion to the Lord. Such godly submission will ensure a sacrifice that will emit the fragrance that is pleasing to God. It will not only be an upright offering that comes out of real servitude towards the family, but will also ensure the flavor or environment of the family.

The husband must present the mandatory or required sacrifice in regard to his marriage. Jesus was the sin or the required sin offering on behalf of His Church. It was His blood that established the New Testament covenant.

In the Old Testament, the sin offering also pointed to the life of an animal being sacrificed as a means to cover the sins. For the husband to honor or prefer his wife's best interests above himself, he must become the mandatory sacrifice to ensure the well-being of the marriage relationship. Although the husband's sacrifice ensures the integrity of the covenant established with his wife, it is a necessary or required sacrifice that will also secure the sanctity of this relationship.

The purpose for covenant in the marriage is to ensure the environment of agreement. This is where the husband and wife walk together, yoked by the same common purpose, goal, and focus in their lives. *Amos 3:3* brings this out. How can two walk together unless there is agreement? Such agreement points to oneness in spirit, intention, and life.

When we consider the oneness or agreement that a married couple should have, we must realize that it points to the fact that marriage is to serve as a living testimony or witness of the reality of Christ and His Church. This is why godly marriages have the potential to be ongoing. They will actually leave an ongoing witness for generations to come. Depending on the length of their lives together, this witness can be made evident and carried forth through the couple's children, grandchildren, and great grandchildren.

This brings us to another important aspect of the Church in regard to being one with Jesus. When Jesus spoke of being one with the Father, He also stated that He was in the Father and the Father was in Him. There is no debate that the Father and Jesus share the same nature, status, and abilities. But, what does it mean for the members of the Church to be in Christ, and Christ in His Body.

Our place in Christ points to our position, but Christ in us points to His life being in us. Positionally, we know that we have been placed in heavenly places with Christ, and that we are actually hid in Him. Since we have been placed in Him, we have all matters that pertain to our spiritual well-being and godliness available to us. The four main virtues of heaven that have been made available in Christ are wisdom, righteousness, sanctification, and redemption.[2]

Once again, "heavenly places" point to our vantage point. We are to consider all matters according to Jesus' wisdom (His Word), in light of His righteousness (His godly examples), through His sanctification (His Spirit), and from His redemption (His work). Such a vantage point will lift us above the envies and jealousies of worldly wisdom, the depravity of personal righteousness, the defilement of the world, and the wretched philosophies of our present age.

Being in Christ reminds us of the environment that we have been placed in to ensure our vantage point. We must never consider matters from a worldly perspective or make conclusions

---

[2] 1 Corinthians 1:30; Ephesians 2:6; Colossians 3:3; 2 Peter 1:3-4

based on introspection according to the self-life. We must be lifted above such limited perceptions in order to see it from the heavenly perspective. Any other perspective will cause great delusion or great bondage.

This brings us to the second aspect of our Christian life, and that is Christ in us. We know that Christ must become our heavenly perception of wisdom, our robe of righteousness, our place of sanctification, and our point of redemption. However, Christ in us speaks of His life.

The members of the true Church of Jesus are identified as living stones that make up a spiritual house, a holy priesthood. The reason that believers are identified in this way is because they possess the very life of Christ. It is His life that makes every believer a living stone, and His Church a living organism, a corporate Body that functions according to its Head.

Although we have already dealt with the subject of how Christians comprise the Church, we have not fully dealt with what it means for the life of Christ to be present in the Church. We know that we are in Christ who must *serve as our all in all* when it pertains to godliness. However, we also must realize that Christ must *be in all aspects of our lives* as a means to possess all that pertains to life.

Consider what the Apostle Paul stated in *Colossians 3:11*, *"Where there is neither Greek nor Jew, circumcision nor uncircumcision, barbarian, Scythian, bond nor free, but Christ is all, and in all."* The real Body of Christ cannot be divided. There may be members of the Church divided, which will cause inconsistencies within local bodies, but the Church of Jesus is not fragmented. His Spirit and life identify each member with His Body. However, as members of this Body, we can see from this Scripture that, regardless of our earthly heritage, our religious status before others, our earthy identity, or our state, it is all about Christ becoming all to, in, and through His Body.

If Jesus is all that the Church is about, our status in the world does not matter. As believers in Christ, we have no real past. We stand equal in importance when it comes to the function of His whole Body. We have no identification other than the Spirit. Our heritage can be traced back to the cross and our spiritual state is that of a bondservant, consecrated unto God for His service.

Christ is not only what the Church should be about, He also must be what the Church becomes. The Church must resonate with His life. He must be the center of every function and activity of His Body. His life must be found in every corner, closet, entryway, room, and court of each member of this living building. He must be found in every decision, practice, and activity.

In essence, the Body must take on the agenda, purpose, and focus of its Head. It must be established in the fullness of Christ's life as each member takes on His likeness. The Apostle Paul brought this out in *Ephesians 4:13, "Till we all come in the unity of the faith, and of the knowledge of the Son of God, unto a perfect man, unto the measure of the stature of the fullness of Christ."*

God's goal was to reveal His Son to the world. In order to do this, He wanted to positionally establish man in the fullness of Christ, so that the life of Christ could fill up every aspect of man with His likeness. The Apostle Paul confirmed this in *Ephesians 1:22-23, "And hath put all things under his feet, and gave him to be the head over all things the church, which is his body, the fullness of him that filleth all in all."*

It is important to point out that the Christian life is complete. We do not possess a partial life of Christ. This complete work and life of Christ was necessary to defeat the complete work of sin and death. Jesus did not just go to the cross; He gave up His life on it. Because of who Jesus is and what He has done, the members of His Church are associated with the word "all".

A good example of this association can be found in *Colossians 1:16-20.* In these Scriptures, we know *all* things are associated with Jesus because He is Creator of *all* things, visible and invisible, along with *all* powers that exist in this world and in the unseen world. He existed before *all* things, and, because of Him, *all* things exist. He is the Head of the Church, the beginning of the first-born of creation that He might have pre-eminence in *all* things. It pleased the Father that in Him should *all* fullness of the Godhead dwell. As a result of His redemption, He has reconciled *all* things unto Himself.

As we consider the word "all," it points to the sum of everything. In Christ, as His saints we have *all* comfort, grace, joy, peace, knowledge, wisdom, revelation, and riches bounding towards us. If we are abiding in love, faith, and obedience, we can be assured that *all* things will work for our good, and that *all* our needs will be supplied to us. We also can trust that *all* of His promises will be brought forth, and that we are heirs with Him in *all* things. Because of our lives in Christ, we know that we can do *all* things through Him.[3]

Obviously, it is God's goal to completely fill Jesus' Church with the fullness of His life. The Apostle Paul confirmed this in *Ephesians 4:10, "He that descended is the same also that ascended up far above all heavens, that he might fill all things."* God is the One who is working in all to bring about this glorious fullness of His Son within His Body.

The Apostle Paul also made this statement in *Ephesians 3:17-19,*

That Christ may dwell in your hearts by faith; that ye, being rooted and grounded in love, May be able to comprehend, with all saints, what is the breadth, and length, and depth, and height, And to know the love of Christ, which passeth knowledge, that ye might be filled with all the fullness of God.

---

[3] Romans 8:28; 15:13-14, 2 Corinthians 1:3, 20; 9:8; Philippians 4:12, 19; Colossians 1:9, 2:2-3; Hebrews 1:2

Clearly, the vision the Church must have is that its main goal must be to possess the fullness of Christ. The fullness of Christ points to the abundant life that He made reference to in *John 10:10*. It is this fullness of His life within the Body that not only establishes complete oneness with the Head and in the Body, but serves as a living testimony of the reality of Christ in the world. It is in this oneness that His life will flow, authority will stand, and power is able to come forth.

Sadly, the visible Church does not display such oneness. In fact, it appears religiously active, but it is lifeless in so many ways. Not only are much of the practices of the visible Church not about Jesus, but they clearly do not display the fullness of His life. As a result, many of the sheep are scattering in search of the fullness that is eluding them. These sheep may not exactly know what they are seeking, but they have a sense of a destiny that is far greater and more encompassing than what they have witnessed.

It is easy to talk about what is wrong with the professing Church, but the challenge is to bring the contrast and heavenly vision to wake it up enough to see its plight. Even though those who are spiritually dulled down may hear words, they will not comprehend, and, although they may see the truth, they will not understand. Sadly, this state will keep these individuals from being converted so that they can be spiritually healed.[4]

What kind of vision do you have in regard to the true Church of Jesus? If you do not have the vision set forth in Scripture, ask the Holy Spirit to revive your heart with this vision.

Such revival will take away any spiritual dullness of compromise from your ears, and to allow the Spirit to put healing salve on any area where there is blindness in your eyes so that you can behold what is in the heart and mind of God. As you allow God to do this incredible surgery on you, consider the real

---

[4] Matthew 13:13-16

challenge set before you as one of the many living stones that have been designated to make up God's spiritual building.

18

DIVIDE AND CONQUER

Jesus taught that a house divided against itself will fall.[1] We know from Scripture that the Church of Jesus is considered both a body and a house. This brings us to an important challenge. We know what happens to a house that is divided, but what happens to a body that finds itself opposing its very function?

It may be hard to understand, but a physical body can turn against itself. In fact, a good indication that a body is turning against itself is allergies. There are known cases where people have become allergic to everything because their bodies were overwhelmed by their inability to function properly.

Regardless of all the activities of the professing Church, it is not functioning according to the Bible. One of the obvious fruits of this malfunction is schisms or divisions. Instead of local churches serving as one Body, most of them have been broken up into separate groups. For example, within a local body, there are the adults who are often being placated with a form of knowledge, but such knowledge rarely brings them to the real knowledge of Jesus.[2]

There are the teenagers who are being presented with a worldly Christianity that is void of truth and holiness. Granted, they are allowed to rock out with ungodly music that stirs up rebellion

---

[1] Matthew 12:25
[2] 2 Timothy 3:7

in the name of Christ, but there is no real semblance of holiness in any of it. These poor young people are not necessarily being prepared to separate themselves from the things of the world that entangle their youthful lusts into the endless web of vanity, defilement, and hopelessness. It appears that in many cases, they are not being challenged to come to terms with a holy God that cannot be seen unless they come to a state of holiness. To come to such a state, they must cease exposing themselves to the silly, foolish, and sensual ways of the world and begin to expose themselves to the power of the uncompromised Word of God.

What about our children? Instead of challenging the foolishness bound up in their hearts, they are being entertained with the foolish things of the world.[3] Our children are becoming so separated from reality that they are not able to distinguish what is real. Thanks to *Veggie Tales*, King David is some silly vegetable who takes on Goliath who is nothing more than a big pickle.

My question is where is the sobriety towards the serious matters of God? As I read the Bible, I wonder how can the older women teach the younger women to be godly if the Body is separated according to personal preference? How can godly men teach the younger men to be godly if they are separated into groups according to age? How can our children understand that they are part of a Body if they are simply being entertained with the rest of the children during Sunday services? How can the different members of the Body find their place in the Body if the Body is not functioning as a Body?[4]

The Bible clearly shows us how the members of Jesus' Body are to function. There are no such worldly practices of separations based on age groups found in the Bible. It is up to the elders to teach the young people how to be godly. Although I have no problem with the concept of Sunday school, I believe that Sunday

---

[3] Proverbs 22:15
[4] 1 Corinthians 12:12, 18-25; 1 Timothy 5:1-2; 1 Peter 5:5

school is not a place of entertainment, but one of teaching our children the seriousness of loving God. However, the concept of children's church is unscriptural.

Children need to learn how to be part of the Body. This is vital if they are to understand order and to learn that they belong to the Body. This will help them to find their place in the Body as they understand that they are a vital part of ensuring not only a healthy Church, but one that also functions correctly according to Scriptural teachings.

In the former fellowship we were overseeing, the children learned what it meant to be part of our Body. The adults of the Body were actively involved in the children's lives. These children were memorizing the books of the Bible, as well as Scriptures that included the Romans' Road in Sunday school. They were encouraged to share what they had learned with the adults and to pray about matters that were affecting the Body. They were constantly being nurtured in the ways of God according to the effectual working of the whole Body.

The youth who were part of the fellowship did not attend a separate Sunday school class. They were part of the adult class where they were expected to learn. They were given Bible Studies to complete during the week, as well as the responsibility of memorizing Scripture weekly. They were also responsible to share these Scriptures with the adults during the Sunday morning class.

They were being brought up in the environment of the Body where they were being equipped to stand strong in order to overcome the wicked one with the Word of God.[5] These young people were involved with decision making in spiritual and administrative matters, as well as evangelism and ministry. As a result, some in the fellowship discovered that God's design for the Body clearly works, if it is properly applied.

---

[5] 1 John 2:13-14

The division that is prevalent in the Church proves the world has been influencing the Church. The more the world influences the philosophies and practices of the professing Church, the more division will occur, not only in the Church, but in families as well. As people identify themselves according to group or denomination, rather than Jesus, or stand on a mixture of theology, rather than truth, and promote religious or worldly practices instead of honorable conduct towards God and others, there will be no real agreement in spirit or truth.

The professing Church is becoming more fragmented. Sadly, what those in this religious system are becoming allergic to as this time draws closer to the end of this present age is the truth. God's truth is actually insulting much of the professing Church. Such truth serves as a sharp sword that will divide asunder the attitude of the soul and the disposition of the spirit. It will expose the workings of the joints and marrow as to the quality of life that is in operation in the Body, and it will reveal the source of wisdom that is inspiring the thoughts, as well as the motivations of the heart.[6]

As the sword exposes the real workings of the professing Church, clear distinction will be made between those who love the truth and those who insist on their own reality concerning the matters of religion.[7] It will divide those who are simply playing church from those who are the Church. It will expose the limitations of denominations and the pettiness of man's doctrine. Ultimately, it will expose who people are truly serving: the Lord of the Church or the god of this present age.

The sword of the Word is constantly coming down in the professing Church. Granted, it is not being brought down by some religious denomination or system; rather, it is being brought down by those who will not compromise the truth of God to fit into the different religious systems or movements. These firebrands will

---

[6] Hebrews 4:12
[7] 2 Thessalonians 2:10-12

not budge from the Rock of ages and from the spirit or intent of the Word of God. Granted, they have their own opinions about different issues, but their faith towards God has established them upon the one true foundation of Christ, lined them up to Him as the cornerstone, and has brought them into maturity or perfection according to His leadership as the Head and Lord of the true Body. They will also not be moved away from the intent or spirit of truth, nor will they agree with another gospel. Like the Apostle Paul, these individuals will insist on integrity in all matters concerning the function of the Body.

It is important to point out that there is a difference between the servants of God who are being led by the Spirit and those who are walking according to their own religious agendas. Those who have their own agendas walk according to their own drumbeat. Such people take pride in the fact that they do not fit into the system, but they also have not really allowed God to place them in the Body. They are doing their own thing.

Such people may possess the truth, but they lack Christian character. Their way of thinking still reveals they are leaning on their own worldly understanding and ways. Therefore, these people may have an understanding of truth, but they do not possess the truth because the attitude and life of Jesus are not prevalent in their approach and conduct when it comes to the matters of life and others. Real servants of God stand out because they are distinct from the world, not because they are proving to be contrary to the religious system.

As the sword of truth comes down, the separation between the light of truth and the delusion of darkness becomes more distinct. Instead of people walking between two opinions, they are being brought to a place of decision and identification. The place of decision comes down to what light they choose to walk according to.[8]

---

[8] 1 Kings 18:21; Joel 3:14; Ephesians 5:8-17; 1 John 1:3-7

The Apostle Paul tells us that Satan also comes as an angel of light. He has his own army of false apostles and ministers who are capable of transforming themselves into a form of righteousness, but their works are bent on destruction. Satan's light is disguised or counterfeited in many ways.

There is the light of self-righteousness for those who want to be the judge, expert, and authority of religious matters, rather than humble, discerning servants in the matters of God. There is the light of knowledge. This arrogant knowledge sees itself as being superior, but it lacks true wisdom and love, revealing the foolishness of this type of light. There is the light of the New Age, where the mind of man is exalted and mystical experiences of the occult are embraced. There is the light of success that considers quantity rather than quality. There is the light of false happiness that encourages every type of pagan, fleshly pursuit to secure a temporary façade of satisfaction.[9]

There is also the light of false religion. Since the Holy Spirit has lifted from the unholy mixture of the world in the professing Church, He has left an empty vacuum that is being filled with every type of Jesus imaginable, as well as worldly practices, methods, and pursuits that have some stamp of religion upon them, but are void of the identifying mark of the Spirit of God and His truth. Obviously, so much of what people perceive to be "Christian" has no life in it.

Since people must have some religious experience to give them a sense of security, there are always those who see the opportunity to capitalize upon such a vacuum. They simply counterfeit what is missing with such things as legalism. Legalism is so oppressive, cruel, bitter, and unrealistic to the spirit that it becomes repulsive.

---

[9] Matthew 7:1-5; 1 Corinthians 8:1-3; 2 Corinthians 11:13-15; 1 Timothy 6:5-   12; Hebrews 5:12-14; James 2:5; 3:13-18

People can also take their religious pursuits to the other extreme of legalism. The other extreme opens the door to doctrines of demons and lying signs and wonders. These counterfeits will fill the insatiable hole with fleshly worship that is totally pagan and experiences that are demonically inspired. These two extremes show scorn towards the real work of the Spirit and prove to despise the real intent of the Bible. Granted, these different approaches use certain parts of the Bible, but, ultimately, they confuse or neglect the real issue of salvation.[10]

Satan does not care what extreme people operate within, just as long as they do not come back to the center of whom God is and His truth. He does not care if such individuals have a whole lot of truth in one area, as long as they do not come into balance where the Spirit or personal conduct is concerned. He does not care if people swing on a high due to a religious spirit, while holding onto some small semblance of truth, as long as they never really discover what it means to experience the Lord in His glory, enabling them to discern their true spiritual condition. He does not care because it is all a form of his worldly darkness that is blinding minds to the true light of Jesus' Gospel.

As you begin to study the condition of the visible or professing Church, you can see three types of environments in operation because of these extremes. Keep in mind that the professing Church is in the boiling pot of the world. Many well-meaning people are being conditioned to regard the matters of God according to a lifeless, twisted, or demonic environment. However, you can find the true Church functioning, even in spite of the boiling pot.

Since we are discussing the Church, let us now consider how it operates according to these environments. First, you have those of the Church who operate as the actual _Body_ of Jesus. This group of people realizes that they must come into one accord to grow up

---

[10] Matthew 23:3-4, 28; 2 Thessalonians 2:8-9; 1 Timothy 4:1-2; Hebrews 2:3

together into the Head. This will ensure that they will properly function as a body according to the vision, plan, and purpose of God. The challenge for the real Body of Jesus is that the members will taste various forms of oppression and persecution since they will not bow down to what is considered normal by the rest of the religious world.

The second group is made up of people who are part of the different _congregations_. People who are part of congregations come together to receive instruction and to worship according to a set schedule or pattern. The problem with many of the people in this particular group is that they maintain their personal identity or selfishness, while settling for some religious environment. In other words, they are not coming together as a means of submitting to one another to ensure the complete function of the Body. They may have agreement with those in the congregation, but they also reserve their right to determine the type of investment, if any, they may make in the kingdom of God.

The final group is made up of people who see themselves as part of the _audience_. These people come to some type of church building to be entertained. They are seeking a "Disneyland" environment to maintain their identity to the world, while being associated with some type of religious experience. Since this form of worldly religion entertains them, they can enjoy what they consider the best of both worlds.

This brings us to the next group of people that must be considered in light of the three groups found in churches—the leaders. The type of leadership that is in place will depend upon the flavor of the group they are overseeing.

Deep calls to deep. You will not find a true servant overseeing an audience any more than you will see the true Body of Jesus accepting a charlatan, performer, or entertainer as its leader. There are three types of leaders. These leaders set up the religious environment that will be prevalent in the local bodies.

Before we address the subject of leaders, let us consider the environments that will be in operation. There are four types of environments. They are classified as fundamental, charismatic, the social club, and that of Spirit and truth. Each environment has its own emphasis. In the fundamental environment, the emphasis is to get back to the basic truths of Christianity. Such an emphasis is sound, but there is one problem, and that is much of it lacks the Spirit. It often proves to be lifeless.

The boundaries for each Christian are Spirit and truth. The Spirit is the one who maintains the integrity of truth. With the Spirit, truth is properly discerned.[11] Without this integrity, such truths will lack life. Truths that lack life will become indifferent, judgmental, and cruel.

A. W. Tozer explained how Fundamentalism fell victim to its own virtues, as the voice of the prophet was silenced by the cult of textualism.[12] Textualism operates according to the same premise as the scribes did in Jesus' day.

Textualism is where man decides how Scripture must be interpreted and understood by those who are being perceived as laity. Instead of touting phylacteries and enlarged borders on their garments as they did in Jesus' day, the scribes of today take pride in their various college degrees.[13]

No doubt, Fundamentalism initially appeared to be an answer to the insanity that was taking place in the religious world, but all it did was establish its own cult mentality as people were made subject to the interpretation of man. Such interpretation of what is truth becomes the superior standard, rather than the simple truths of the Bible. It is from this premise that all spiritual matters are judged.

---

[11] John 4:23-24; 16:13; 1 Corinthians 2:10-16
[12] Keys to the Deeper Life; A. W. Tozer, © 1957, 1984 by Creation House; Clarion Classics, Published by the Zondervan Publishing House, pg. 19
[13] Matthew 23:5

Once again, we are reminded that the ways of man and the world never really change. The religious system that put man in bondage during Jesus' day still exists; only it is being sold under the guise of Fundamentalism to the laity. The deeds and doctrines of the Nicolaitans of Revelation are now being sold to Christians through Replacement Theology. As Solomon tells us, there is nothing new under the sun.[14] In Christendom, we can find repackaged heresy that is always being sold under new names and titles.

This brings us to the Charismatic movement. This movement swung in the opposite direction from Fundamentalism. This is where the finger pointing comes into play. You have the Fundamentalists calling the Charismatic people insane and ridiculous. You have the Charismatic people calling the Fundamentalists dead and judgmental. Who is correct? Sadly, both can prove to be correct.

The Charismatic movement sought after spirit in order to have evidence of some spiritual life and experiences. However, in some cases there was no discernment of the spirit that was coming through the door. It did not seem to matter whether the spirit in operation was lining up to the Word of God. As a result, the antichrist spirit came in with various New Age and occult experiences. Since these experiences seemed so real, many embraced them as being reality.

Out of this unholy mixture came methods and practices that the professing Church has embraced. Such methods and practices include Positive Confession and visualization. However, the latest practice in this long line of ungodly exercises that has been paraded and exalted through each antichrist movement in the Christian realm is contemplative prayer.

The next environment is the social club. Clearly, those of the Fundamental and the Charismatic camps would never come into

---

[14] Ecclesiastes 1:9

agreement. They are poles apart in their emphasis. Hence, welcome the emergent church.

The emergent church is nothing more than a big social club with a "Disneyland" atmosphere. The emergent church plays both sides of the two religious poles by not insulting anyone. For example, the truth and Gospel are presented in an extremely watered-down state, but it will satisfy the mentality of those who are seeking some form of religious truth.

To satisfy the other group, the true Spirit has been counterfeited in the worship service. Therefore, on one side is the Fundamentalist who hears a semblance or appearance of the truth along with the Gospel being alluded to, and, on the other side, there are ample opportunities for those in the Charismatic camp to have a satisfying emotional experience. As a result, both groups can happily sit in the boiling pot of the world with some semblance of agreement at the expense of both Spirit and truth. Needless to say, the environment that is being established by the emergent church is ushering in the one-world religious system under the guise of Social Justice that will fall under the complete control of the antichrist spirit.

The latest movement are the "Real Life Churches." They promote relationship with God, which is all well and good, but I am not sure the authority is there. People must be born again. Relationship can't save you, and you can't have a relationship with God unless Jesus is the head and cornerstone of the Church.

I am sure there are pastors in this movement that are called and are inspired from above, but the ones I have encountered avoid controversial issues that the Bible clearly addresses such as sin in the camp, the Holy Spirit, the end times, and dire warnings. They appear to fit in with the world, instead of stand distinct in it. They believe in elders but avoid the pastoral position. In some cases, they proudly tout that they are an "elder only" church but such leadership is not scriptural.

I realize God can use anything to bring in heirs. However, my main concern with wrong emphasis, weak presentations of the Gospel, Christian calling, and holy living is that the sheep may not be prepared to stand, and the leaders will answer for it.

This brings us to the final environment: that of Spirit and truth. The integrity of truth is upheld in this environment to ensure that the Holy Spirit has freedom to move upon hearts and lives as He imparts, prepares, teaches, and guides the Body of Christ. Souls are saved, lives are changed, and people are healed and restored. This is where true worship occurs and service is defined and often becomes sacrificial for the glory of God.

It is within these environments that you can also find different types of leadership. There are the true shepherds of Jesus, the hireling shepherds, and the wolves. Within the first three environments, you will find that the true leaders (shepherds) are either frustrated, stifled, or in despair as they must constantly contend for the faith that was first delivered to the saints. Some of these leaders are actually being abused and driven out of some of the local churches.

There are also the hireling shepherds and wolves who will see the first three environments as platforms on which to fulfill their personal agendas, as they strive to undermine the Spirit and integrity of truth in the fourth environment. Sometimes, these false shepherds manage to split a local body in their attempt to gain control over the sheep. Needless to say, the real flock of God will find itself in the middle of a chess game, where the members perceive themselves as being pawns. Let us now consider how these three types of leaders operate.

The real shepherd has a distinct heart, calling, and emphasis. This shepherd's heart is towards the Lord and His sheep. The Chief Shepherd, Jesus Christ, has called this individual into this position. Out of loving devotion for the true Shepherd and with deep humility, meekness, and trepidation, this shepherd will always lead the sheep towards the reality of Jesus. This shepherd is not in competition with the Chief Shepherd, for this committed leader has one goal, and that is God must be glorified in His fold.

The true shepherd knows that, unless the sheep learn to hear the voice of their Chief Shepherd, they will never know a satisfying life. This humble shepherd is not in this vocation because of money, importance, or prestige, but because of the calling and the faithfulness that comes out of loving and knowing the Chief Shepherd. The main responsibility of this shepherd will serve as this individual's constant emphasis and pursuit, and that responsibility is to feed the sheep of God to ensure spiritual maturity.[15]

The hireling shepherd comes in many forms. The many different seminaries have formed many of these imposters. Sadly, these seminaries, with their mixtures of theology and worldly philosophies, such as Psychology, produce what we call cookie-cutter ministers that often promote atheistic, amoral, New Age, and liberal views. In other words, they have been cut out of the same worldly or religious cloth.

These individuals may start out with a call, but, because of the non-inspired, worldly influence that has invaded much of the professing Church's way of thinking, such callings can be drowned out by skepticism and unbelief. Such individuals are like those of Ephraim. They become a half-baked cake that has never been turned and baked on the other side. On one side, they look like they may have the spiritual goods to lead the people of God, but, on the other side, there is carnality, pride, and immaturity.[16]

Being a pastor to the Body of Christ is both a calling and a vocation. However, the calling can be defiled and confused by the ways of the world, and the vocation replaced by the wrong emphasis. Wrong emphasis will lack the right heart. Ultimately,

[15] John 10:4; 1 Peter 5:1-4
[16] Hosea 7:8-15; Colossians 2:8

such misdirected emphasis often embraces the attitude of the subculture that we refer to as Christianity to hide immature, fleshly devotion. As such a person loses heart, they will become blinded by the philosophies and practices of the world that have been packaged as acceptable Christian practices.

Hireling pastors often end up feeding the flock with what I call placebo truths that are surrounded by a worldly emphasis. Worldly emphasis will change the intent of truth as it feeds the sheep sugar-coated poisons of heresy.

Wrong spiritual diets always strip the truth of its power and authority to impact others and will ultimately rob the professing Church of life as it causes it to become sluggish. Such shepherds become void of godly concern for the flock and its spiritual growth. Eventually, the real sheep will become disillusioned because they do not hear the voice of the true Shepherd coming forth out of the mouth of these false shepherds. They will eventually scatter as they seek pastures that are satisfying, and clean water that is able to revive them once again.[17]

Wolves are different from hireling shepherds because their main goal is to seek a following. The hireling shepherd often sees God's flock as an opportunity to do good or make a difference. Since their motive is self-serving, such shepherds end up fleecing the sheep or abandoning them altogether to become prey to the wolves. However, a wolf sees the flock as a means to survive. These individuals seek out the sheep to not only fleece them, but to also use them to feed their overrated ego. If the poor sheep fail to serve the purpose of the wolf, they will taste the hatred and cruelty of these leaders.

In their delusion, such wolves perceive that it is the sheep's responsibility to sacrifice all to meet their personal desires and agendas, rather than the other way around. Granted, they will throw bones at the miserable little creatures to keep them

---

[17] Ezekiel 34; John 10:1-5

unaware of what is really happening around them, but these wolves have no intention of serving the sheep. Ultimately, they will sacrifice the sheep who refuse to follow them, as well as condition those who do follow into obeying only their voice, making them two-fold the children of hell that they are themselves.[18]

Those who are strong sheep will confront these heretics with the Word of God.[19] However, if the wolf fails to repent, then all sheep must flee from the leadership of such a self-serving, cruel, unreasonable individual.

This brings us to the Word of God. The unbelief of the *world* will always attack or undermine the authority of the Word. The skepticism of man will always downplay the ways of faith towards the validity of the Word by perverting or applying the Word in an unrealistic way. In such an environment, the Word never becomes personal so that those hearing or receiving it can clearly discern their own spiritual condition. Rather, it becomes judgmental towards others.

Worldly knowledge will make the Word appear obsolete or metaphoric, rather than absolute. Spiritualizing the things of God will make the truth of the Word appear inferior when considered in its unadulterated form. Obviously, the Word of God has been misused, abused, and neglected. It is often being presented lightly, as "fluff" if you will, rather than in the salty form that brings contrast to heal wounds, as well as necessary judgment or separation. It has been sugar-coated with misinterpretation, rather than allowed to serve as the sharp two-edged sword that reveals the vanity and frivolous ways of such interpretations. It has been paraphrased according to the popular winds of the time and translated according to the environment of the age (generally from Gnostic sources that our spiritual forefathers rejected as fables).

---

[18] Matthew 7:15; 10:16; John 10:8-10
[19] Titus 3:10-11

In each worldly, uninspired paraphrase and translation of God's Word, the spirit or intent has been changed to cover up the insidious handling of it.[20] These attempts have a goal, and that is to condition God's people to embrace the unholy mixture of the world with the things of God. These unholy mixtures cleverly render the powerful Christian life into a worldly subculture that fits nicely into the various activities of the world. [21]

As for the *wolves,* they will use the Word as a blindfold or a club. In other words, they will cleverly use the Word as a means of blinding the sheep to their real intentions, all the while changing the intent of Scripture to subtly line their poor followers up to their way of thinking. If the sheep fail to line up to their leaders' insane reality, the leaders will use the Word as a club to beat them into total subjection to their abominable leadership, often leaving the poor sheep wounded and in total despair.

The *hireling* shepherds will twist the Word to give the impression that they are feeding the sheep, but, in reality, there is no real substance behind any of it. In the end, the sheep will fall victim to malnutrition. Such sheep often become prey to the winds of false doctrines and the various wolves that present themselves as apostles, prophets, and ministers of righteousness.

As you study these different environments in operation, you can see how they result in division. In the _Body_, the division comes when the Father prunes away the members that are void of any real life or fruit.[22]

For those in the _congregations_, the division comes when the wind blows through their ranks. The wind can be that of the Holy Spirit who serves as the fire that will test and purify the believers to reveal their real level of devotion. Or, it could be the wind of

---

[20] 2 Timothy 2:15

[21] If you would like to understand how to properly divide the Word of truth, see the author's book, *My Words Are Spirit and Life* in Volume 1 of the Foundation series.

[22] John 15:1-8

persecution that will purge to bring distinction between those who are standing on the Rock and those who are standing on the shifting sands of self-righteousness. Finally, there are also the winds of false doctrines that will sweep away those who are unstable into the tidal wave of delusion.[23]

God simply turns the _audiences_ of the professing Church over to their lusts. There is no place of real conviction because the glory of God's holiness has been changed into the latest form of entertainment. It is hard to say how much of the knowledge of the true God is retained in such an environment, but, if there are any sheep in such a place, eventually they will have to repent and come out and be separate from the charade.[24]

As you can see, the professing Church is being divided in various ways, but what about the true Church of Jesus? Is it being divided, refined, and/or defined by the separation that is taking place in the professing Church? More importantly, what division do you belong to?

Are you part of the Body, being established according to the leadership of the Head? Perhaps, you are part of a congregation that has gone through some challenges and separation. Maybe, you have fallen into the lie and façade of being part of the popular audiences. It is time to make sure you are truly part of the universal Church that is neither limited by walls, nor defined by denomination or established by man's doctrine. Rather, your identification is truly in Christ in light of His wisdom, with Him in His righteousness, through His sanctification due to the work of the Spirit, and according to His work of redemption.

---

[23] Matthew 7:24-27; John 16:8; Acts 2:1-21; Ephesians 4:14; 2 Thessalonians 2:3, 10-12; 2 Timothy 3:12
[24] Romans 1:23-25; 2 Corinthians 6:14-18; Hebrews 12:14

19

THE GATES OF HELL
WILL NOT PREVAIL

Whatever happened to the Church? We know that the face of the professing Church has changed according to the different winds that have blown through the ages. For me, in my initial Christian years, it was all about denomination. The most asked question was, "What denomination, or I should say "particular religious box", do you belong to?" This was so that you could be classified as being Fundamental, Charismatic (Pentecostal), or Liberal. In today's age of mega-churches and the endless stream of false apostles and prophets hitting the scene with their own brand of heresy, the popular question when this book was written was, "Who is your covering?"

Regardless of the latest or newest question, the real concern, in most instances, is not about one's soul; rather, it is about whether you fit into the newest presentation of the latest wind of worldly, lifeless, and uninspired non-sense that is taking the professing Church by storm. Much of the visible Church appears as if it does not care if you are on your way to eternal damnation. All it seems to care about is that you do not go against the grain of its worldly systems, controlled arenas, and delusions that are presently in operation.

Clearly, as the professing Church is conditioned by the different winds of the doctrines of man and demons that blow through Christendom, it is becoming more allergic to the unadulterated truth of the Bible. In fact, some of those professing to be Christians would not recognize the Biblical presentation of what true Christianity constitutes any more than they would recognize the true Jesus of the Bible.

The question we must now pose is whatever happened to the true Church of Jesus? Obviously, the true Church constitutes the saints that truly have received the life of Jesus and have maintained that life by faith.

As you study the lives of these saints, the answer to what has happened to the true Church is quite simple and obvious. From the time the world started coming into the midst of the professing Church and gaining a foothold into its way of thinking, the real Church has been continually coming out from the influence of the world and becoming separate from the religious system.

The true Church continues to discover the same truth: *it can never change the environment of the world, but the world can change it.* Therefore, the members of the true Church are constantly separating from the influence of the age they are living in to ensure their status as God's children, kings, and priests.[1] As a result, they have consistently proved to be worthless to the world, insulting and irritating to the religious system, and immovable when assaulted by the changing winds of doctrine of both men and devils.

Members of this true Church of Jesus are being constantly challenged to discover true Christianity in the midst of the counterfeits. Most blood-bought saints start out being part of the professing Church. In their initial Christian lives, they are told what to think, how to conduct themselves, and what is true. But eventually, as they grow in Christ, they find themselves hitting the

---

[1] John 1:12; 2 Corinthians 6:14-18; Revelation 1:6

ceiling of their denomination and knocking their heads against doctrine that is an ungodly mixture void of life, godly love, and revelation.

Even in the midst of this conditioning, the saints sense a stirring of the Spirit within them. There is a realization that there is so much more to this incredible life. At first, they fumble in their search, but, eventually, they begin to realize what that more is. It is more of God.

Once they recognize that their true desire is to see, know, and experience the fullness of their Lord and the life He has for them, they begin to recognize the signs of leanness in their spirit that are being unveiled to them. They will begin to see that the leanness is caused by the limitations of man and the defilement of the world.

Such leanness of spirit will eventually become unbearable to these individuals. Therefore, some of these believers find themselves stepping outside of the "box." Granted, they usually find themselves in another "box," but at least the next "box" allows them a bit more room to explore the unlimited depths of their infinite God from a different perspective that has more depth to it.

Once these seeking saints encounter the limitation of the next "box", their restlessness will fan into a flame, causing them to come out and be even more separated. They eventually discover that their sincere desire to know God leads them on an incredible journey. This journey leads them into secret places where they begin to experience Him. It also takes them through the barren wilderness of the present age.

In this barren wilderness, these saints discover that the religious attempts and experiences of man can only bring them so far in their spiritual search. As they begin to see that the light of denominations and traditions will eventually restrict their present growth, they quickly find themselves in another barren place, where they must choose to cling to the Rock. These stout, hearty individuals refuse to be cut out of the same religious cloth as others have been. They want to find their own place, identity, and life in Jesus. This identity will not be based on some denominational box that is inadequate or some movement that is clearly moving outside of the Scriptural boundaries of the Word of God.

The restlessness in the spirit of these individuals is the Holy Spirit, always calling them outside of limitations in order to come higher in their lives in Christ. However, such a journey will take them into valleys of despair. God must go deeper in a person's character before they can come higher in his or her life with Him.

These individuals may be sitting in congregations, but they have developed a secret life in God that makes them distinct in ways that cannot be explained. They may be in a group of religious people, but these individuals will never really belong to the group, for they continue to travel the course that God has prepared for them. Their walk of faith will lead them outside of the camp of religion with its traditions and activities into the wilderness of preparation.[2] In essence, these individuals are always being prepared to meet God in their incredible journey, in spite of the darkness of the present age.

This brings us to the statement that Jesus made in *Matthew 16:18, "And I say also unto thee, That thou art Peter, and upon this rock (Jesus) I will build my church, and the gates of hell shall not prevail against it."* (Parenthesis added.)[3] The professing Church may have changed throughout the ages, but the real Church of Jesus remains the same. Although hell may do all it can to replace the work of the Holy Spirit, redefine the foundation of Jesus, adjust the cornerstone of who He is, and make true faith worthless with unholy agreements, misdirected loyalties, and alliances, the true Church never moves from the Rock that it has clearly been established upon. Granted, it may become confused,

---

[2] 2 Timothy 4:7; Hebrews 13:10-14
[3] 1 Corinthians 10:4

oppressed, and occasionally lost in the midst of the onslaught of counterfeit presentations, but it will always come back to the Rock.

The reason the true Church will come back to the Rock of ages, is because its heart will not be satisfied unless it is lined up to the cornerstone. The spirit of the true Church will not settle for a different faith because nothing else makes sense outside of Jesus as its Head (His leadership), serving as its Vine (the source of life), partaking of Him as its Bread (the place of nourishment and communion), and being firmly established on Him as its Foundation (knowing and experiencing spiritual stability).

The true Church of Jesus has a clear understanding that the Lord has redeemed it.[4] It does not belong to itself. It does not represent self-interests. It is not here to be popular or to fit into this world. It stands upon truth, regardless of how unpopular. It also withstands with truth, regardless of the possible rejection and persecution it may experience, and it is always determined to stand because of truth, regardless of the extent of darkness that is invading the souls of others. It is here to function according to the leadership, life, and purpose of Jesus Christ. In Him, this unique Body that is known as the Church stands complete. But, without Him, the Church knows it is void of life and purpose.

The Apostle Paul gave us insight into what the true Church of Jesus has been experiencing for the past 20 centuries. He made this statement in *2 Corinthians 4:7-11,*

> *But we have this treasure in earthen vessels, that the excellency of the power may be of God, and not of us. We are troubled on every side, yet not distressed; we are perplexed, but not in despair; Persecuted, but not forsaken; cast down, but not destroyed; Always bearing about in the body the dying of the Lord Jesus, that the life also of Jesus might be made manifest in our body. For we who live are always delivered unto death for Jesus'*

---

[4] 1 Corinthians 6:17-20; 7:22-24

sake, that the life also of Jesus might be made manifest in our mortal flesh.

Members of the Body who truly gain a sense of who they are in Christ realize they are simply clay vessels. As vessels formed by the influences of the world, the members of Christ' Body are aware that they were found by God to be marred vessels. Marred by sin, they had to be purged. The only way they could be purged was to be broken so that the Potter could once again take them through a process that would make them sanctified vessels that could possess the priceless gift of the life of Jesus.[5]

For the saint who understands the necessity for such a process, they are humbled by it. In humility, the members of the Body of Christ realize that the Christian walk is contrary to what is nominal and acceptable, even to the religious world. A. W. Tozer best described the type of creature that saints become in his book *The Radical Cross.*

Tozer pointed out that the saints will put themselves in jeopardy in order to be safe in Christ. To save their lives, they will lose them. They humble themselves so that they can be lifted up. They are strongest when they are the weakest. They are spiritually poor so they can make others rich. They possess the most after they have given most everything away. They experience the heights of God when they are the lowest. They are more aware of sin when they are sinless in their walk. They know the most when they realize they know nothing outside of Jesus. For the saints, the most is accomplished when they are standing still before the Lord, waiting for His instruction. In heaviness they manage to rejoice as they keep their hearts in the state of gladness during times of grave sorrow.[6]

---

[5] Leviticus 11:32-33; Jeremiah 18:1-4; 2 Timothy 2:19-21

[6] The Radical Cross: Living the Passion of Christ; A. W. Tozer, © 2005 by Zur Ltd; pg. 102

Tozer explained that the real character of Christians is being revealed constantly in their attitude towards salvation. They believe they are saved presently, but they expect to be saved later and look forward to a future salvation. These individuals fear God, but do not live in fear of Him.

In God's presence they feel overwhelmed and totally exposed, but there is no place they would rather abide. They know that they have been cleansed from sin, but they are keenly aware that they have nothing to offer Him according to their flesh. Although they are lowly, they know what it means to talk to the King of kings. Even though they are aware of being insignificant, they also know how important they are to God.[7]

It is such an attitude that makes the members of Jesus' Body vessels that are trustworthy to carry the prize possession of His life everywhere they go. They are like the woman who anointed Jesus for His burial. They are always ready to be sacrificially broken at the feet of Jesus so others can experience the fragrance of His sweet life. [8]

For this reason, the true Body of Jesus stands distinct. This distinction can cause its members to experience trouble from all sides. Satan stirs up such trouble to wipe out the reflection of Jesus' life. If need be, he stirs up the religious people with jealousy, inspires the world to placate sin by offering up the truth with flattery, bullying, or persecution, and blinds the masses to the fact that they are being led as sheep to the slaughter, while rejecting and crucifying the truth.[9] However, in such trouble, the true Body of Christ will not give way to the distress that may encamp about them.

Granted, the Body will surely become perplexed by the mocking attitudes and actions of those who claim to be religious

---

[7] Ibid, pg. 103
[8] Matthew 26:6-13; 2 Corinthians 2:14-16
[9] Isaiah 53:6

or godly. The members of His Body will also struggle with the unpredictable opposition that accompanies these individuals as they resist the truths and ways of God in the name of Jesus, for the cause of love or with their notions of righteousness. Even though reasoning may elude these saints as to the insanity that often operates in the name of religious righteousness, they will not allow themselves to wallow in despair.

In many parts of the world, the true Church tastes the bitter sweetness of persecution. On one hand, the members of this eternal Body marvel that all false religions of the world fear Christianity. If these deluded persecutors' perception is true, why fear a simple message of the Gospel?

However, these enemies of Christianity do fear it because it represents truth. Such truth will set the captive free from the clutches of religion and various delusions. Therefore, these false religions must snuff out the light of true Christianity. However, the more they try, the greater the light burns in the hearts of those who love and know their Lord. These saints know that the Lord will never forsake them in their time of persecution.

Some members of the Church are being cast down into the miry pits of rejection and oppression. Like the prophet Jeremiah, they will faithfully and obediently labor in these dark pits because of their faith towards God and His Word. Ultimately, their bodies may be destroyed, but their souls will be preserved by the faithfulness of God. These individuals are assured of a better resurrection. They will know that it is through such sanctifying fires that the Church of Jesus will be refined and presented as a Body without spot and wrinkle.[10]

The Apostle Paul also reminded us in *Romans 8:36-37, "As it is written, For thy sake we are killed all the day long; we are accounted as sheep for the slaughter. Nay, in all these things we are more than conquerors through him that loved us."* Once again,

---

[10] Jeremiah 18:19-23; Matthew 10:28; Ephesians 5:27; Hebrews 11:35

we are reminded that, as believers, we must become identified with Jesus in His death, burial, and resurrection. The apostle explained in *2 Corinthians 4:11-12* that death is always working in each of us as the servants of God. We are bearing in our life of worship and service the reality of Jesus' death on our behalf. Therefore, we are constantly being led to the slaughter so that His life can manifest itself in and through our bodies. It is all about His glory being reflected in our very countenance.[11]

The Bible is clear that God always has a remnant that will remain true to Him, regardless of the darkness of the present age that is invading the hearts and minds of people. These saints will not bow to Baal in any way. They will not give honor or preference to any idolatrous altar. They may be weary behind the closed doors of their hidden life in Christ, but they will remain true. They will stand distinct from the world as strangers and pilgrims in spite of the rejection and persecution. Like Peter, these saints realize that there is no other to whom they can turn who has eternal life.[12] As a result, they cling faithfully to Jesus as they rest in His glorious hands.

In this place of abiding, they will stand firmly upon Him as their foundation; they will continue to line up to Him as the precious cornerstone, find abiding joy in His Word, and know that He is the source of their unwavering faith. Ultimately, they will be able to claim and verify the promise that Jesus gave His disciples in *Matthew 16:18*, which is, the very gates of hell will not prevail against His Church.

Is this your claim? Are you a member of the true Church of Jesus? Perhaps you are limited by some type of "box," but are restless in your soul. Seek God as to what you must do in your particular barren wilderness. God may call you aside, apart, or into a secret place with Him.

---

[11] Romans 12:1; 2 Corinthians 3:18
[12] John 6:68-69

Maybe you see that the particular doctrine that you have been established in lacks real power and revelation; therefore, you are ready to rethink what you have been conditioned to believe. If so, put aside what you think you know and understand, approach the Bible to believe it, and ask the Spirit to give you God's perspective.

You might even be someone who is in a religious environment that makes no sense, but you do not know where to go. Flee to God and asked Him for more of Himself. Come under His Spirit and be led to those pastures and waters that will satisfy your hungry soul.

Remember, the great cloud of witnesses proves that, since we are God's people, we do not have to settle for a substandard existence or accept lifeless religious presentations or an inconsistent life. We do not have to become part of the subculture of the professing Church to simply belong. We do not have to allow the winds of the present age to influence us.

As believers, we can find our lives in Christ as we are established on the foundation, defined according to the cornerstone, and free to discover the unfeigned faith that was first delivered to the saints. Perhaps, in the darkness of the present age we live in, we will develop a life that God considers a sweet sacrifice that even the world is not worthy of witnessing and tasting.

The bottom line is that, as a believer, it is your life, your choice, and your sacrifice. When all is said and done, you alone will answer for what you did with the life of Christ that was so wonderfully entrusted to you as one of the many members of His living, eternal, universal Body, the Church.

Bibliography

Strong's Exhaustive Concordance of the Bible; James Strong, © 1986 assigned to World Bible Publishers, Inc

Webster's New Collegiate Dictionary; © 1976 by G. & C. Merriam Co.

Deeper Experience Of Famous Christians; by James Gilchrist Lawson; © 2000 by Barbour Publishing Inc.

The Four Hundred Silent Years; H. A. Ironside; 16th printing 1980; Loizeaux Brothers

A Glimpse at Early Christian Church Life; Tertullian, © 1991 by David W. Bercot

Nicolaitanism (The Rise and Growth of the Clergy), F. W. Grant, Believers Bookshelf Inc.

Smith's Bible Dictionary; William Smith, Thomas Nelson Publishers

A Woman Rides the Beast; © 1994 by Dave Hunt, Published by Harvest House Publishers

Keys to the Deeper Life; A. W. Tozer, © 1957, 1984 by Creation House; Clarion Classics, Published by the Zondervan Publishing House

The Radical Cross: Living the Passion of Christ; A. W. Tozer, © 2005 by Zur Ltd.

Lectures on Colossians; H. A. Ironside; 15TH printing, May 1978; Published by Loizeaux Brothers, Inc.

The Pilgrim Church; Edmund Broadbent; © 1999, Gospel Folio Press

You Will Receive Power, William Law; © 1997 by Whitaker House

Other books by Rayola Kelley:

Volume Six: Developing Our Christian Life
The Many Faces of Christianity
*Possessing Our Souls
Experiencing the Christian Life
The Power of Our Testimonies
*The Victorious Journey

Devotions
Devotions of the Heart: Books One and Two
Daily Food for the Soul: Books One and Two

Gentle Shepherd Ministries Devotion Series:
Being a Child of God
Disciplining the Strength of our Youth
Coming to Full Age

Nugget Books:
Nuggets From Heaven
More Nuggets From Heaven
Heavenly Gems
More Heavenly Gems
Heavenly Treasures
More Heavenly Treasures

Gentle Shepherd Ministries Series:

The Christian Life Series
What Matter Is This?
The Challenge of It
The Reality of It

The Leadership Series
Overcoming
A Matter of Authority and Power
The Dynamics of True Leadership

Books By:

Jeannette Haley

Books co-authored with Rayola Kelley:
Hidden Manna (original)
The Many Faces of Christianity (Volume 6)
Post to Post 3: Meditations Along the Way
Post to Post 4: Inspirations Along the Way
Post to Post 5: Collecting Gems Along the Way

Other Books:
Rose of Light, Thorn of Darkness
Interview In Hell}
Interview On Earth}
(Both Interview Books are now in one book
Angelus Assignments)
The Pig and I
Reflections of Wonder (Devotional)

Children's Books:
Little Stories for Little People
Traveler's Tales
The Adventures of Zack and Mira
The Adventures of Paul and Dana
(A House on the Beach)
The Monster of Mystery Valley

*Books that have been separated from the volumes and are now available under their own titles.

www.ingramcontent.com/pod-product-compliance
Lightning Source LLC
Chambersburg PA
CBHW061044110426
42740CB00049B/1811